Knockout

Knit Hats and Hoods

Knockout

Knit Hats and Hoods

30 engaging designs for beanies, tams, slouches, and more

Diane Serviss

STACKPOLE
BOOKS

Guilford, Connecticut

Published by Stackpole Books
An imprint of The Rowman and Littlefield Publishing Group, Inc.
4501 Forbes Blvd., Ste. 200, Lanham, MD 20706
www.rowman.com

Distributed by NATIONAL BOOK NETWORK
800-462-6420

Model photography by Gale Zucker
Technique photography by Diane Serviss

We have made every effort to ensure the accuracy and completeness of these instructions. We cannot, however, be responsible for human error, typographical mistakes, or variations in individual work.

British Library Cataloguing in Publication Information available

Library of Congress Cataloging-in-Publication Data

Names: Serviss, Diane, author.
Title: Knockout knit hats and hoods : 30 Engaging Designs for Beanies, Tams, Slouches, and More / Diane Serviss.
Description: First edition. | Guilford, Connecticut : Stackpole Books, [2018] | Includes index.
Identifiers: LCCN 2018025415 (print) | LCCN 2018026521 (ebook) | ISBN 9780811768146 (ebook) | ISBN 9780811717663 (pbk. : alk. paper) | ISBN 9780811768146 (e-book)
Subjects: LCSH: Knitting—Patterns. | Hats.
Classification: LCC TT825 (ebook) | LCC TT825 .S463 2018 (print) | DDC 746.43/2—dc23
LC record available at https://lccn.loc.gov/2018025415

First Edition
Printed in the United States of America

Contents

Introduction

I believe with all my heart that knitters are not just craftspeople, we are artists; our hands careworn by the miles of yarn that travel through them. We lay the groundwork and labor on it stitch by stitch until simple, raw, and wholesome materials are transformed into cozy masterpieces. We paint landscapes, sculpt childhood memories, illustrate exotic locales—all from the comfort of our favorite chair. The very best part of knitting is that we can share the products of this art and even the skills of creating this art with each other.

Like any artist, my work reflects my own experiences, the places I have been and the people I am privileged to know. I have found inspiration in the quaint Vermont country setting where I grew up, the welcoming sandy beaches of Florida where I now reside, and all the mountains and milestones between. This collection of patterns represents snapshots of my life, moments in time captured in wool.

How to Use This Book

How to Read a Pattern

When deciding on a pattern, it is best to read all the instructions first, from beginning to end. Be sure it is suitable for your needs and offers the size you'll require or an explanation of how to alter it. Note the yarn and other supplies called for. Take into consideration the stitches and techniques employed in the pattern, and your level of comfort with them. That being said, do not limit yourself. Acquiring a new skill is often just a short lesson away. Tutorials such as those offered in this book are incredibly useful, and there is also a bounty of information to be found on the Internet.

Some patterns in this book include charts and color grids. As all of these patterns are written to be knit in the round, the charts should be read from right to left, bottom to top, as you will always be working on the right side of the fabric. It is assumed that the pattern will be repeated to complete each round. Pattern stitch charts will include a chart key where each symbol represents a specific type of stitch.

Sizing

Each pattern begins with an indication of what size head the finished garment should fit, as well as the measurements of the finished piece lying flat and unstretched. Some patterns include instructions for more than one size. Where multiple sizes are not available, I recommend going up or down a needle size to accommodate a different circumference.

Gauge

Gauge refers to the number of stitches and rows per inch in a particular pattern stitch while using a specific sized knitting needle and yarn.

It is always best to knit your own swatch using the same combination of needle and yarn or a similar yarn substitution as referenced in the pattern. Use a tape measure or gauge tool to compare your stitch and row count to those suggested in the pattern. If the same gauge is not met, increase or decrease the size of the needle to counteract those differences.

Also, be aware that you might not hit gauge spot-on, as everyone knits with a different tension, both across and vertically. What's most important for fit is that the number of stitches per inch matches the gauge. If you've hit the stitch gauge but your gauge on rows is off—either more rows per inch or less rows per inch than what is called for—you can fix that by adding or subtracting rows when knitting the body of the hat.

Needles and Tools

Knitting needles come in various sizes and materials, as well as three types: straight, double-pointed, and circular. I most often design in the round using circular needles, and therefore I rarely use straight needles; even when knitting a flat piece, I tend to still knit on circulars, without joining. Each pattern will indicate the type and size needed, but the material they are made of is your choice.

Circular knitting is a way of knitting a tube that has no seams. When casting on your stitches, be careful not to twist the stitches on your foundation row before joining the stitches and always place a marker between the first and last stitches to mark the end of each round. As you're decreasing, switch to double-pointed needles before the knitting becomes too tight on the circular needle.

Other basic tools you will need include stitch markers, scissors, a yarn needle, a cable needle, and a ruler or gauge tool.

Yarn and Yarn Substitution

Patterns not only require a certain weight of yarn, but many patterns are only successful if the right texture and color are used, as well. Dark yarns, for example, can mask cable details. Some yarns are highly textured, have a fuzzy halo, or have a strong variegated-color pattern and are not appropriate for patterns with a raised-stitch detail. A smooth single-ply or multi-ply yarn that is not prone to splitting often works best for patterns that require sharp stitch definition. Often your designer has already done the legwork for you, choosing a type of yarn that is the right fit for the pattern.

If a yarn substitution is needed or desired, be certain to choose something that does not stray too far from the original. All of the information you will need is located on the yarn label. A checklist of things to be mindful of includes:

1. Yarn weight: The thickness of the yarn is referred to as yarn weight. There are seven yarn weights (as designated by the Craft Yarn Council)—the higher the number, the heavier the yarn. Thinner yarns require smaller needles and will produce more stitches per inch; heavier yarns require larger needles and produce fewer stitches per inch. It is important to choose a yarn in the same weight class as intended in the pattern to produce a somewhat predictable amount of stitches per inch.

2. Length per skein: Length is typically measured in yards and/or meters. Be careful to purchase enough yarn for the entire project. Better to have a little too much than not enough. In every pattern, I tell you the exact yardage the hat requires, so you don't end up getting caught short if you're substituting another yarn with a different skein length.

3. Dye lot: When purchasing multiple skeins of yarn, make certain they all come from the same dye lot, which will be stamped

on the label. The same number means they were dyed in the same batch, ensuring the color with be consistent from skein to skein. Skeins from different dye lots can vary in shade. An ombre look can be a nice design detail when intentional, but a real disaster when it's not.

4. Fiber content: Yarn is made from a wide range of materials, from wool to cotton to acrylic to blends of multiple fibers and more. Each fiber offers a different durability, ease of care, drape, and feel. When substituting a different yarn for the one originally intended, look for similarities in these characteristics. Novelty yarns are rarely a good choice for a knitted garment and should be reserved for accents.

5. Needle suggestion and gauge: You will notice a square yarn symbol on the label of each skein of yarn. It will include the suggested needle size (for both knitting and crochet) to use with this yarn, and the number of stitches and rows this combination should create when knitted in stockinette pattern. Do not solely rely on this information; you should still swatch your yarn as indicated in each of my patterns before beginning your project to ensure proper gauge.

6. Care instructions: Basic care instructions are usually included on the yarn ball band. They will let you know whether the yarn should be exclusively hand-washed or if it is machine washable, like a super-wash wool. If it says to hand-wash, please do, or you'll likely end up with a felted hat.

When it comes to quality and price, I always recommend buying the best quality of yarn in your price range that meets the characteristics needed for the pattern. After all, if you're going to spend time creating the project, it would be a pity if your efforts were not long-lasting or simply lost in translation because of a poor yarn choice. Luxurious yarn, however tempting, is not always the best choice, and lesser-priced yarns are not always the worst choice. That is to say, not all yarns are created equal, nor are all yarns suitable for every pattern, and price should only be one factor in the decision.

Blocking and Washing

Blocking your knits is a necessary step that many knitters overlook. Although it is more important for natural fibers than synthetics, blocking your knits helps to smooth out any inconsistencies in the stitches and bloom the yarn. When a project is finished, I suggest holding it over a steaming pot of water or misting it with a spray bottle. You may then either lay it flat to dry or position it over a balloon blown up to roughly your head size. Berets can be dried over a ten-inch dinner plate to give them a saucer effect. Avoid overstretching the ribbing.

To hand-wash your knits, fill a basin with lukewarm water and add a mild detergent or yarn soak if desired. Avoid agitation and wringing; instead, you should pat and lightly press. Allow your knits to soak for a few minutes, then gently rinse the garment, supporting it so it does not stretch. Roll the garment in a towel, jellyroll style, to pull out the remaining moisture. Lay the item flat to dry; do not allow it to hang.

Beanstalks Slouchy Hat

With its spritely color and trendy chevron lacework, Beanstalks is a bright reminder of spring. This hat has a modern slouch and a soft, stretchy brim, perfect for today's laid-back style. This one-skein project will stay vibrant all year, no green thumb required!

FINISHED MEASUREMENTS
Circumference at brim band, unstretched: 17 in (43 cm); will fit head circumference of 20 to 23 in (50.5 to 58 cm)
Length from brim edge to crown: 9½ in (24 cm)

YARN
150 yd (137 m) worsted weight #4 yarn; shown knitted in #0055 Baby Lettuce, Willow Yarns Burrow Worsted, 75% acrylic, 25% wool, 197 yd (180 m) and 3.5 oz (100 g) per skein

NEEDLES AND OTHER MATERIALS
- One 16-in (40.5 cm) circular knitting needle, US 7 (4.5 mm) or size needed to obtain gauge
- US 7 (4.5 mm) set of 5 double-pointed needles or size needed to obtain gauge
- Stitch marker
- Scissors
- Yarn needle

GAUGE
20 sts x 28 rows in Stitch Pattern = 4-in (10 cm) square

STITCH PATTERN
Rnd 1: *K1, yo, ssk, k7, k2tog, yo, k1, p1; rep from * around.
Rnd 2: *K13, p1; rep from * around.
Rnd 3: *K2, yo, ssk, k5, k2tog, yo, k2, p1; rep from * around.
Rnd 4: *K13, p1; rep from * around.
Rnd 5: * K3, yo, ssk, k3, k2tog, yo, k3, p1; rep from * around.
Rnd 6: *K13, p1; rep from * around.
Rnd 7: *K4, yo, ssk, k1, k2tog, yo, k4, p1; rep from * around.
Rnd 8: * K13, p1; rep from * around.

Rnds 1–12: *K1tbl, p1; rep from * around.
Rnd 13: K13, p1; rep from * around.

Body

Rnds 1–40: Following chart or written instructions, work entire Stitch Pattern 5 times.

Crown Shaping

Rnd 1: *K1, ssk, k7, k2tog, k1, p1; rep from * around—84 sts.
Rnd 2: *K11, p1; rep from * around.
Rnd 3: *K1, ssk, k5, k2tog, k1, p1; rep from * around—70 sts.
Rnd 4: *K9, p1; rep from * around.
Rnd 5: *K1, ssk, k3, k2tog, k1, p1; rep from * around—56 sts.
Rnd 6: *K7, p1; rep from * around.
Rnd 7: *K1, ssk, k1, k2tog, k1, p1; rep from * around—42 sts.
Rnd 8: *K5, p1; rep from * around.
Rnd 9: *Ssk, k1, k2tog, p1; rep from * around—28 sts.
Rnd 10: *K3, p1; rep from * around.
Rnd 11: *Sl1k, k2tog, psso, p1; rep from * around—14 sts.

Finishing

Cut yarn, leaving an 8-in (20.5 cm) tail. Thread yarn needle with end and pick up remaining stitches on knitting needles. Pull tightly to close and secure end. Weave in yarn tails on inside of hat.

NOTES

- Hat is worked in rounds from bottom edge to crown. Switch from circular needles to double-pointed needles when necessary during crown shaping.

Brim

Using long-tail method and circular needle, CO 98 sts. Place a stitch marker between first and last sts and join in the round, being careful not to twist the cast-on row.

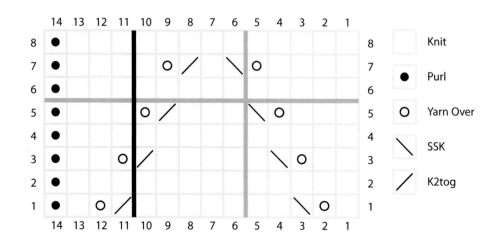

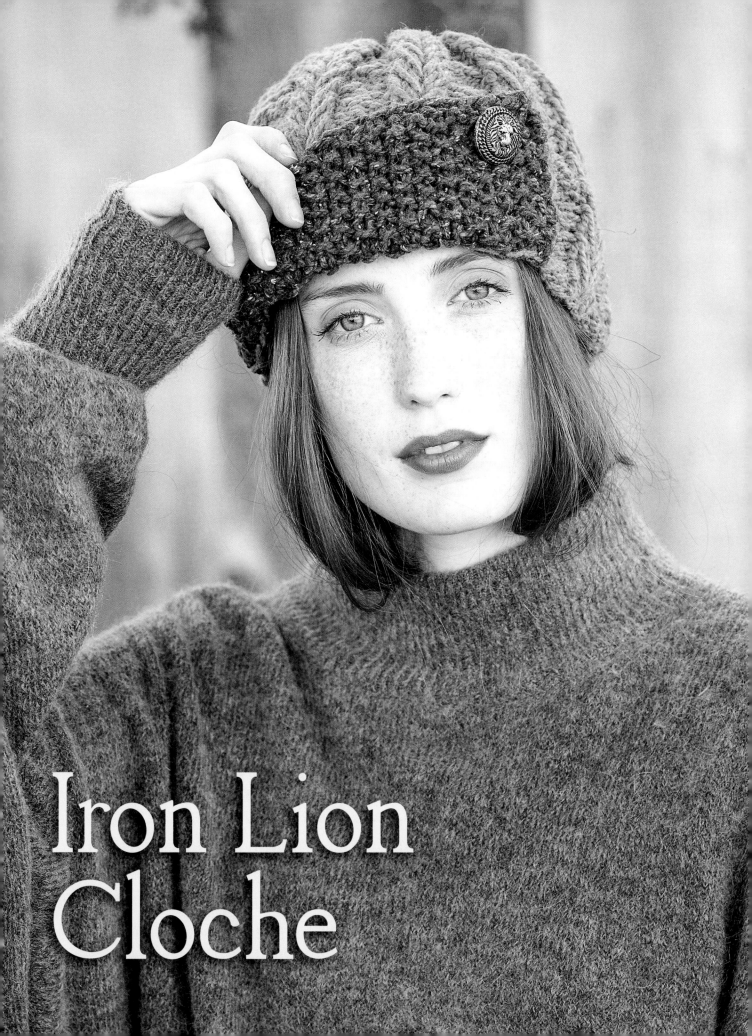

Iron Lion Cloche

A juxtaposition between nature and industry, wholesome rows of grain are interrupted by a brim overlay detail. The wool and silk blend yarn provides depth with its smattering of tweedy bits and flecks. A strong button with a vintage feel ties the look together.

FINISHED MEASUREMENTS

Small/Medium:

Circumference at brim band, unstretched: 18 in (46 cm); will fit head circumference of 20 to 21½ in (50.5 to 55 cm)
Length from brim edge to crown: 7¾ in (20 cm)

Large/Extra-Large:

Circumference at brim band, unstretched: 20 in (51 cm); will fit head circumference of 21½ to 23 in (55 to 58 cm)
Length from brim edge to crown: 7¾ in (20 cm)

YARN

Small/Medium:

MC: 98 yd (90 m) bulky weight #5 yarn
CC: 8 yd (7 m) bulky weight #5 yarn

Large/Extra-Large:

MC: 108 yd (99 m) bulky weight #5 yarn; shown knitted in #05 Golden, Cascade Yarns Tivoli, 60% wool, 40% silk, 109 yd (100 m) and 3.5 oz (100 g) per skein
CC: 8 yd (7 m) bulky weight #5 yarn; shown knitted in #10 Navy, Cascade Yarns Tivoli, 60% wool, 40% silk, 109 yd (100 m) per skein

NEEDLES AND OTHER MATERIALS

- One 16-in (40.5 cm) circular knitting needle, US 10 (6.0 mm) or size needed to obtain gauge
- US 10 (6.0 mm) set of 5 double-pointed needles or size needed to obtain gauge
- Stitch marker
- Scissors
- Yarn needle
- Large button

GAUGE

11 sts x 24 rows in Stitch Pattern using US 10 (6.0 mm) needles = 4-in (10 cm) square

SPECIAL STITCHES

Elongated loop left (elL): Insert right needle into center of second knit stitch of previous three knit rib four rows below. Wrap the right needle with the working yarn counterclockwise. Pull up a loop of working yarn onto the right needle.

Elongated loop right (elR): Insert right needle into center of second knit stitch of next three knit rib four rows below. Wrap the right needle with the working yarn counterclockwise. Pull up a loop of working yarn onto the right needle.

Purl 3 together decrease (p3tog): Insert the right needle into the first three stitches on the left needle. Purl these stitches together as though they are one stitch.

STITCH PATTERN

Rnd 1: *ElR, k3, elL, p3; rep from * around—72 (80) sts.
Rnd 2: *Sl1p, k3, sl1p, p3; rep from * around.
Rnd 3: *Sl1k, k1, psso, k1, k2tog, p3; rep from * around—54 (60) sts.
Rnd 4: *K3, p3; rep from * around.

NOTES

- Hat is worked in rounds from bottom edge to crown. Switch from circular needles to double-pointed needles when necessary during crown shaping.
- Decorative flap will be made by picking up and knitting stitches along the cast-on edge and knitting flat.
- Stitch counts for Large/Extra-Large size will be shown in parentheses.
- For photo tutorials on working the elongated loop stitches and purl 3 together decrease, see pages 118 and 122.

Brim

Using long-tail method and US 10 (6 mm)
  circular needle, CO 54 (60) sts in MC. Place
  a stitch marker between first and last sts and
  join in the round, being careful not to twist
  the cast-on row.
Rnds 1–4: *K3, p3; rep from * around.

Body

Rnds 1–36: Work entire Stitch Pattern 9 times.

Crown Shaping

Rnd 1: *Sl2k, k1, psso, p3; rep from *
  around—36 (40) sts.
Rnd 2: *K1, p3; rep from * around.
Rnd 3: *K1, p3tog; rep from *
  around—18 (20) sts.
Rnd 4: *K1, p1; rep from * around.
Rnd 5: *K2tog; rep from * around—9 (10) sts.

Finishing

Cut yarn, leaving an 8-in (20.5 cm) tail. Thread
  yarn needle with end and pick up remaining
stitches on knitting needles. Pull tightly to
close and secure end. Weave in yarn tails on
inside of hat.

Decorative Flap

With brim facing away and leaving an 8-in
  (20.5 cm) long tail for sewing, pick up and
  knit 21 (27) sts along the front loops only of
  the cast-on edge using CC. Do not join in
  the round.
Row 1 (RS): *K1, p1; rep from * until last
  stitch, k1.
Row 2: K2tog, *k1, p1; rep from * until last stitch,
  k1—20 (26) sts.
Row 3: *K1, p1; rep from * until last 2 sts, k2tog—
  19 (25) sts.
Row 4: K2tog, *k1, p1; rep from * until last stitch,
  k1—18 (24) sts.
Rows 5–16: Repeat rows 3 and 4 until 6 (12)
  sts remain.
Bind off, leaving a 12-in (30 cm) tail for sewing.
  Thread yarn needle with end and sew right
  edge of flap to hat. Sew left short edge of
  flap to hat. Attach large button to upper
  right corner of flap. Weave in yarn tails on
  inside of hat.

Twisting
Streams Beret

This classic cabled beret features a right-leaning twist repeat that is easy to memorize. Choose a rich, solid-colored yarn that will not mask the tightly packed motif. Resist the carefree urge to spin around and toss it into the air when wearing it.

FINISHED MEASUREMENTS

Circumference at brim band, unstretched: 17 in (43 cm); will fit head circumference of 20 to 23 in (50.5 to 58 cm)
Length from brim edge to crown: 8½ in (22 cm)

YARN

190 yd (173 m) worsted weight #4 yarn; shown knitted in #M82 Blue Flannel, Brown Sheep Company Lamb's Pride Worsted, 85% wool, 15% mohair, 190 yd (173 m) and 4 oz (113 g) per skein

NEEDLES AND OTHER MATERIALS

- One 16-in (40.5 cm) circular knitting needle, size US 7 (4.5 mm) or size needed to obtain gauge
- One 16-in (40.5 cm) circular knitting needle, size US 10½ (6.5 mm) or size needed to obtain gauge
- US 10½ (6.5 mm) set of 5 double-pointed needles or size needed to obtain gauge
- Cable needle
- Stitch marker
- Scissors
- Yarn needle

GAUGE

22 sts x 22 rows in Cable Stitch Pattern using larger needle (US 10½ [6.5 mm] needle or size needed to obtain gauge) = 4-in (10 cm) square

SPECIAL STITCHES

3/3 right cross (3/3 RC): Slip next 3 sts to cable needle, hold cable needle to back of work, knit 3 sts from main needle, knit 3 sts from cable needle.

Make 1 left (M1L) increase: Insert the left needle from front to back into the horizontal strand between the stitches on the right and left needles. Knit the lifted loop through the back.

NOTES

- Hat is worked in rounds from bottom edge to crown. Switch from circular needles to double-pointed needles when necessary during crown shaping.
- This pattern will require the entire skein of yarn. Be mindful of excess wastage at the cast-on.
- For photo tutorials on working 3/3 right cross and make 1 left increase, see pages 113 and 120.

Brim

Using long-tail method and US 7 (4.5 mm) circular needle, CO 96 sts. Place a stitch marker between first and last sts and join in the round, being careful not to twist the cast-on row.

Rnds 1–12: *K1, p1; rep from * around.

Rnd 13: Using US 10½ (6.5 mm) circular needle, *k2, M1L; rep from * around—144 sts.

Body

Rnds 1–3: *K6, p1, k1, p1; rep from * around.

Rnd 4: *3/3 RC, p1, k1, p1; rep from * around.

Rnds 5–11: *K6, p1, k1, p1; rep from * around.

Rnd 12: *3/3 RC, p1, k1, p1; rep from * around.

Rnds 13–19: *K6, p1, k1, p1; rep from * around.

Rnd 20: *3/3 RC, p1, k1, p1; rep from * around.

Rnds 21–27: *K6, p1, k1, p1; rep from * around.

Rnd 28: *3/3 RC, p1, k1, p1; rep from * around.

Crown Shaping

Rnd 1: *K2tog, k4, p1, k1, p1; rep from * around—128 sts.

Rnd 2: *K2tog, k3, p1, k1, p1; rep from * around—112 sts.

Rnd 3: *K2tog, k2, p1, k1, p1; rep from * around—96 sts.

Rnd 4: *K2tog, k1, p1, k1, p1; rep from * around—80 sts.

Rnd 5: *K2tog, p1, k1, p1; rep from * around—64 sts.

Rnd 6: *K2tog, k1, p1; rep from * around—48 sts.

Rnd 7: *K2tog, p1; rep from * around—32 sts.

Rnd 8: *K2tog; rep from * around—16 sts.

Finishing

Cut yarn, leaving an 8-in (20.5 cm) tail. Thread yarn needle with end and pick up remaining stitches on knitting needles. Pull tightly to close and secure end. Weave in yarn tails on inside of hat.

Dewdrops
Beanie

This project is a great introduction into simple lace knitting. A clever, controlled drop-stitch design creates a fabric with great movement and texture. Neat, offset columns mimic droplets of dew streaming down a window pane.

FINISHED MEASUREMENTS

Small/Medium:

Circumference at brim band, unstretched:
   16 in (41 cm) unstretched; will fit head
   circumference of 20 to 22 in (50.5 to 56 cm)
Length from brim edge to crown: 8 in (20 cm)

Large/Extra-Large:

Circumference at brim band, unstretched: 16½
   in (42 cm); will fit head circumference of 22 to
   23 in (56 to 58 cm)
Length from brim edge to crown: 8 in (20 cm)

YARN

Small/Medium: 100 yd (91 m) worsted
   weight #4 yarn

Large/Extra-Large: 120 yd (110 m) worsted
   weight #4 yarn; shown knitted in #6294
   Turquoise Mix, Berroco Ultra Alpaca, 50%
   alpaca, 50% wool, 215 yd (198 m) and 3.5 oz
   (100 g) per skein

NEEDLES AND OTHER MATERIALS

- One 16-in (40.5 cm) circular knitting
  needle, US 8 (5.0 mm) or size needed to
  obtain gauge
- US 8 (8.0 mm) set of 5 double-pointed
  needles or size needed to obtain gauge
- Stitch marker
- Scissors
- Yarn needle

GAUGE

20 sts x 24 rows in Drop Stitch Rib = 4-in
   (10 cm) square

Brim

Using long-tail method and circular needle, CO 88 (96) sts. Place a stitch marker between first and last sts and join in the round, being careful not to twist the cast-on row.

Rnds 1–5: *K2, p2; rep from * around.
Rnd 6: *K1, yo, k1, p2, k2, p2; rep from * around—99 (108) sts.

Body

Rnds 1–24: Work entire Drop Stitch Rib pattern twice.

Crown Shaping

Rnd 1: *K3, p2, k2, p2; rep from * around.
Rnd 2: *K3, p2, k2tog, p2; rep from * around—88 (96) sts.
Rnd 3: *K3, p2, k1, p2; rep from * around.
Rnd 4: *K3, p2, k1, p2tog; rep from * around—77 (84) sts.
Rnd 5: *K3, p2, k1, p1; rep from * around.
Rnd 6: *K1, drop 1, k1, p2, k1, p1; rep from * around—66 (72) sts.
Rnd 7: *K2, p2, k1, p1; rep from * around.
Rnd 8: *K2, p2tog, k1, p1; rep from * around—55 (60) sts.
Rnd 9: *K2, p1, k1, p1; rep from * around.
Rnd 10: *K2tog, p1, k1, p1; rep from * around—44 (48) sts.
Rnd 11: *K1, p1; rep from * around.
Rnd 12: *K1, p1, k2tog; rep from * around—33 (36) sts.
Rnd 13: K1, *p1, k2; rep from * around to last 2 sts, p1, k1.
Rnd 14: *K2tog, k1; rep from * around—22 (24) sts.
Rnd 15: Knit.
Rnd 16: *K2tog; rep from * around—11 (12) sts.

Finishing

Cut yarn, leaving an 8-in (20.5 cm) tail. Thread yarn needle with end and pick up remaining stitches on knitting needles. Pull tightly to close and secure end. Weave in yarn tails on inside of hat.

STITCH PATTERN

Drop Stitch Rib:

Rnds 1–5: *K3, p2, k2, p2; rep from * around.
Rnd 6: *K1, drop 1, k1, p2, k1, yo, k1, p2; rep from * around.
Rnds 7–11: *K2, p2, k3, p2; rep from * around.
Rnd 12: *K1, yo, k1, p2, k1, drop 1, k1, p2; rep from * around.

NOTES
- Hat is worked in rounds from bottom edge to crown. Switch from circular needles to double-pointed needles when necessary during crown shaping.
- Stitch counts for Large/Extra-Large size will be shown in parentheses.

Wildflower
Fields Beanie

Panels of stockinette mingle with columns of slipped stitches to create this elegant beanie. Simple crown shaping leads to a mock pleated gather. This quick project is ideal for showcasing smooth hand-painted and kettle-dyed yarns.

FINISHED MEASUREMENTS

Small/Medium:

Circumference at brim band, unstretched: 16 in (41 cm); will fit head circumference of 20 to 21 in (50.5 to 53 cm)
Length from brim edge to crown: 7¾ in (20 cm)

Large/Extra-Large:

Circumference at brim band, unstretched: 17 in (43 cm); will fit head circumference of 22 to 23 in (56 to 58 cm)
Length from brim edge to crown: 8¼ in (21 cm)

YARN

Small/Medium: 110 yd (100 m) worsted weight #4 yarn; shown knitted in #621 Deja Vu, Malabrigo Worsted Merino Yarn, 100% merino wool, 210 yd (192 m) and 3.5 oz (100 g) per skein

Large/Extra-Large: 130 yd (119 m) worsted weight #4 yarn

NEEDLES AND OTHER MATERIALS
- One 16-in (40.5 cm) circular knitting needle, US 7 (4.5 mm) or size needed to obtain gauge
- US 7 (4.5 mm) set of 5 double-pointed needles or size needed to obtain gauge
- Stitch marker
- Scissors
- Yarn needle

GAUGE
18 sts x 30 rows in Stockinette Stitch = 4-in (10 cm) square

STITCH PATTERN

Rnd 1: Knit.
Rnd 2: *Sl1k, k7; rep from * around.

NOTES

- Hat is worked in rounds from bottom edge to crown. Switch from circular needles to double-pointed needles when necessary during crown shaping.
- Stitch counts for Large/Extra-Large size will be shown in parentheses.

Brim

Using long-tail method and US 7 (4.5 mm) circular needle, CO 88 (96) sts. Place a stitch marker between first and last sts and join in the round, being careful not to twist the cast-on row.
Rnds 1–14: *K1, p1; rep from * around.

Body

Rnds 1–28 (32): Work entire Stitch Pattern 14 (16) times.

Crown Shaping

Rnd 1: Knit.
Rnd 2: *Sl1k, k5, k2tog; rep from * around—77 sts (84 sts).
Rnd 3: Knit.
Rnd 4: *Sl1k, k4, k2tog; rep from * around—66 sts (72 sts).
Rnd 5: Knit.
Rnd 6: *Sl1k, k3, k2tog; rep from * around—55 sts (60 sts).
Rnd 7: Knit.
Rnd 8: *Sl1k, k2, k2tog; rep from * around—44 sts (48 sts).
Rnd 9: Knit.
Rnd 10: *Sl1k, k1, k2tog; rep from * around—33 sts (36 sts).
Rnd 11: Knit.
Rnd 12: *Sl1k, k2tog; rep from * around—22 sts (24 sts).
Rnd 13: Knit.
Rnd 14: *K2tog; rep from * around—11 sts (12 sts).

Finishing

Cut yarn, leaving an 8-in (20.5 cm) tail. Thread yarn needle with end and pick up remaining stitches on knitting needles. Pull tightly to close and secure end. Weave in yarn tails on inside of hat.

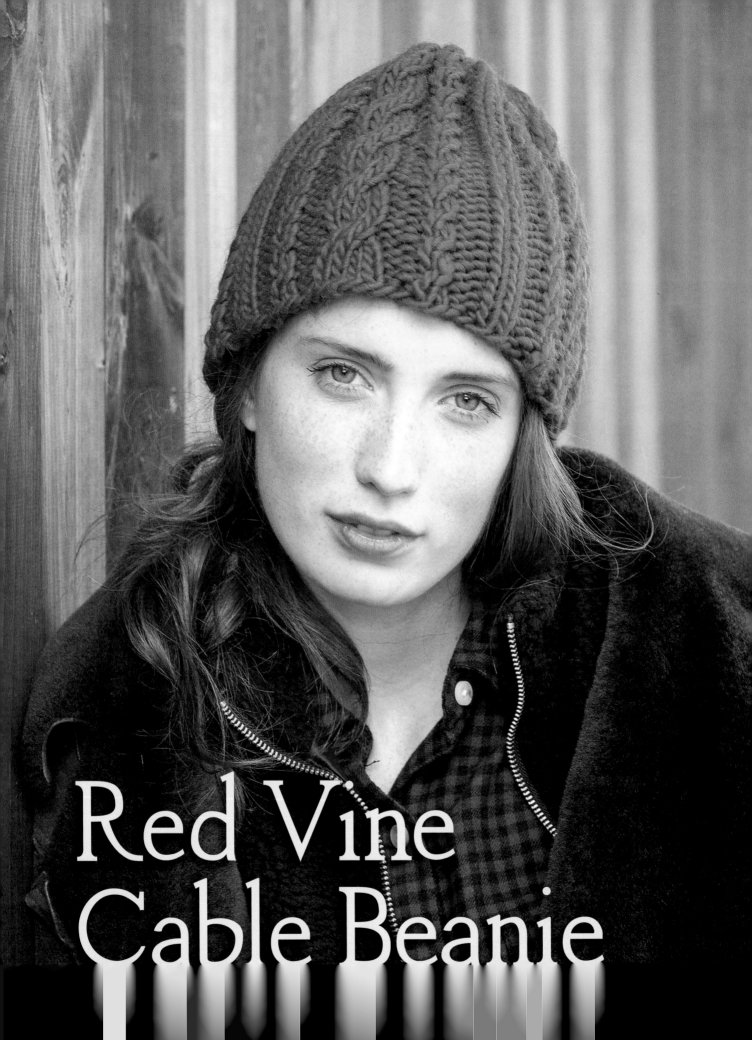

Red Vine
Cable Beanie

An exercise in twists and turns, this hat is the perfect practice vehicle for knitting cables. It is a one-skein, one-evening project that looks much more complicated than it truly is. Knit in a stunning red, it is unisex and a great last-minute gift.

FINISHED MEASUREMENTS
Circumference at brim band, unstretched: 18 in (46 cm); will fit head circumference of 20 to 23 in (50.5 to 58 cm)
Length from brim edge to crown: 8½ in (22 cm)

YARN
110 yd (101 m) bulky weight #5 yarn; shown knitted in #M080 Blue Blood Red, Brown Sheep Company Lamb's Pride Bulky, 85% wool, 15% mohair, 125 yd (114 m) and 4 oz (113 g) per skein

NEEDLES AND OTHER MATERIALS
- One 16-in (40.5 cm) circular knitting needle, US 10½ (6.5 mm) or size needed to obtain gauge
- US 10½ (6.5 mm) set of 5 double-pointed needles or size needed to obtain gauge
- Stitch marker
- Cable needle
- Scissors
- Yarn needle

GAUGE
15 sts x 18 rows in Cable Stitch Pattern = 4-in (10 cm) square

SPECIAL STITCHES
Right twist (RT): Insert the right needle into second stitch on the left needle knitwise. Wrap the working yarn around the right needle counterclockwise. Pull the working yarn through the stitch, leaving the stitch on the needle. Insert the right needle into the first stitch on the left needle knitwise. Wrap the working yarn around the right needle counterclockwise. Pull the working yarn through the stitch, sliding both stitches off the left needle.
2/2 right cross (2/2 RC): Slip next 2 sts to cable needle, hold cable needle to back of work, knit 2 sts from main needle, knit 2 sts from cable needle.

Cable Stitch Pattern:

Rnds 1–2: *K2, p2, k4, p2, k2, p2, k2, p2; rep from * around.

Rnd 3: *RT, p2, k4, p2, RT, p2, k2, p2; rep from * around.

Rnds 4–5: *K2, p2, k4, p2, k2, p2, k2, p2; rep from * around.

Rnd 6: *RT, p2, 2/2 RC, p2, RT, p2, k2, p2; rep from * around.

NOTES

- Hat is worked in rounds from bottom edge to crown. Switch from circular needles to double-pointed needles when necessary during crown shaping.
- For a photo tutorial on working 2/2 right twist and right cross, see pages 111 and 112.

Brim and Body

Using long-tail method and circular needles, CO 72 sts. Place a stitch marker between first and last sts and join in the round, being careful not to twist the cast-on row.

Rnds 1–30: Work entire Cable Stitch Pattern 5 times.

Crown Shaping

Rnds 1–2: *K2, p2, k4, p2, k2, p2, k2, p2; rep from * around.

Rnd 3: *RT, p2, k4, p2, RT, p2, k2, p2; rep from * around.

Rnd 4: *K2tog, p2, k2tog twice, p2, k2tog, p2, k2tog, p2; rep from * around—52 st.

Rnd 5: *K1, p2tog, k2tog, p2tog, k1, p2tog, k1, p2tog; rep from * around—32 sts.

Rnd 6: *K2tog; rep from * around—16 sts.

Rnd 7: *K2tog; rep from * around—8 sts.

Finishing

Cut yarn, leaving an 8-in (20.5 cm) tail. Thread yarn needle with end and pick up remaining stitches on knitting needles. Pull tightly to close and secure end. Weave in yarn tails on inside of hat.

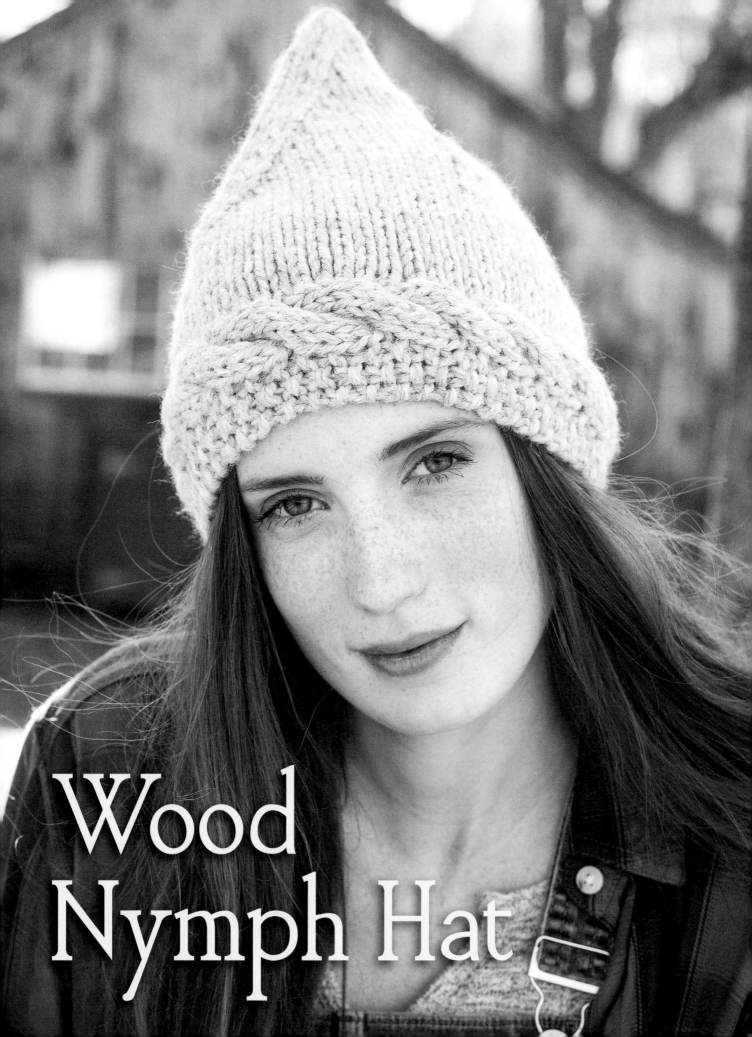

Wood Nymph Hat

Pointy hats aren't just for elves and garden gnomes! This whimsical beanie is a playful addition to any winter wardrobe. A cabled pattern around the brim takes this hat from ordinary to extraordinary.

FINISHED MEASUREMENTS

Small/Medium:

Circumference at brim band, unstretched: 18 in (46 cm); will fit head circumference of 20 to 22 in (50.5 to 56 cm)

Length from brim edge to crown: 10½ in (27 cm)

Large/Extra-Large:

Circumference at brim band, unstretched: 19 in (48 cm); will fit head circumference of 22 to 23 in (56 to 58 cm)

Length from brim edge to crown: 11 in (28 cm)

YARN

Small/Medium: 85 yd (78 m) bulky weight #5 yarn; shown knitted in #630-188 Mulberry, Lion Brand Wool-Ease Chunky, 80% acrylic, 20% wool, 153 yd (140 m) and 5 oz (140 g) per skein

Large/Extra-Large: 95 yd (87 m) bulky weight #5 yarn; shown knitted in #630-155 Silver Grey, Lion Brand Wool-Ease Chunky, 80% acrylic, 20% wool, 153 yd (140 m) and 5 oz (140 g) per skein

NEEDLES AND OTHER MATERIALS

- One 16-in (40.5 cm) circular knitting needle, US 10½ (6.5 mm) or size needed to obtain gauge
- US 10½ (6.5 mm) set of 5 double-pointed needles or size needed to obtain gauge
- Stitch marker
- Cable needle
- One US J-10 (6 mm) crochet hook
- Scrap yarn
- Scissors
- Yarn needle

GAUGE

12 sts x 16 rows in Stockinette Stitch = 4-in (10 cm) square

SPECIAL STITCHES

3/3 right cross (3/3 RC): Slip next 3 sts to cable needle, hold cable needle to back of work, knit 3 sts from main needle, knit 3 sts from cable needle.

STITCH PATTERN

Cable Stitch Pattern:

Row 1 (WS): P1, k1, p8.
Row 2: K7, p1, k1, p1.
Row 3: P1, k1, p8.
Row 4: K1, 3/3 RC, p1, k1, p1.
Row 5: P1, k1, p8.
Row 6: K7, p1, k1, p1.

NOTES

- Hat begins by knitting a cable stitch brim band. Stitches are then picked up around the band. Remainder of hat is worked in rounds from brim edge to crown. Switch from circular needles to double-pointed needles when necessary during crown shaping.
- Stitch counts for Large/Extra-Large size will be shown in parentheses. When only one count is given, it applies to both sizes.
- For photo tutorials on working provisional crochet cast-on, 3/3 right cross, and Kitchener stitch, see pages 104, 113, and 126.

Brim

Using scrap yarn, the crochet hook, and one of the double-pointed knitting needles, CO 10 sts using provisional crochet cast-on method. Crochet 4 chain sts after cast-on row to easily unravel scrap yarn later. Switch to working yarn, knit first row into live sts on needle.

Rows 1–94 (100): Using double-pointed needles, work entire Cable Stitch Pattern 15 (16) times. Then work rows 1–4 of Cable Stitch Pattern.

Break yarn, leaving 8-in (20.5 cm) tail. Untie provisional cast-on row scrap yarn and, using free needle, pick up the live stitches from provisional cast-on row. Remove scrap yarn. Thread yarn needle with tail. With wrong sides of the knitted fabric facing each other, use the Kitchener stitch to seamlessly join the live stitches together.

Body

Using circular needle, pick up 56 (60) stitches around the top cable edge of brim band.
Rnds 1–12: Knit.

For Large/Extra-Large size only:

Rnd 13: *K13, k2tog; rep from * around—56 sts.
Rnd 14: Knit.

Crown Shaping

Rnd 1: *K12, k2tog; rep from * around—52 sts.
Rnd 2: Knit.
Rnd 3: *K11, k2tog; rep from * around—48 sts.
Rnd 4: Knit.
Rnd 5: *K10, k2tog; rep from * around—44 sts.
Rnd 6: Knit.
Rnd 7: *K9, k2tog; rep from * around—40 sts.
Rnd 8: Knit.
Rnd 9: *K8, k2tog; rep from * around—36 sts.
Rnd 10: Knit.
Rnd 11: *K7, k2tog; rep from * around—32 sts.
Rnd 12: Knit.
Rnd 13: *K6, k2tog; rep from * around—28 sts.
Rnd 14: Knit.
Rnd 15: *K5, k2tog; rep from * around—24 sts.
Rnd 16: Knit.
Rnd 17: *K4, k2tog; rep from * around—20 sts.
Rnd 18: Knit.
Rnd 19: *K3, k2tog; rep from * around—16 sts.
Rnd 20: Knit.
Rnd 21: *K2, k2tog; rep from * around—12 sts.
Rnd 22: Knit.
Rnd 23: *K1, k2tog; rep from * around—8 sts.
Rnd 24: Knit.
Rnd 25: *K2tog; rep from * around—4 sts.

Finishing

Cut yarn, leaving an 8-in (20.5 cm) tail. Thread yarn needle with end and pick up remaining stitches on knitting needles. Pull tightly to close and secure end. Weave in yarn tails on inside of hat.

Lake
Bonnet

A beginning knitter's dream, this hat is knit flat. Simple construction makes for a tranquil, no-fuss project. With its comfortable, easy fit and deep-layered garter ridges, this bonnet is a great way to avoid "hat hair," while keeping your ears warm and toasty.

FINISHED MEASUREMENTS

Small/Medium:

Circumference at widest edge of bonnet, unstretched: 15 in (38 cm); will fit head circumference of 20 to 21½ in (50.5 to 55 cm)
Length from bottom edge to center top: 9 in (23 cm)

Large/Extra-Large:

Circumference at widest edge of bonnet, unstretched: 16 in (41 cm); will fit head circumference of 21½ to 23 in (55 to 58 cm)
Length from bottom edge to center top: 9½ in (24 cm)

YARN

Small/Medium: 110 yd (101 m) bulky weight #5 yarn

Large/Extra-Large: 120 yd (110 m) bulky weight #5 yarn; shown knitted in #7449 Lake McDonald, Berroco Lodge, 47% wool, 47% acrylic, 6% rayon, 98 yd (90 m) and 1.75 oz (50 g) per skein

NEEDLES AND OTHER MATERIALS
- One 24-in (61 cm) circular knitting needle, US 10½ (6.5 mm) or size needed to obtain gauge
- US 10½ (6.5 mm) set of 2 double-pointed needles or size needed to obtain gauge
- Stitch marker
- Scissors
- Yarn needle

GAUGE
14 sts x 26 rows in Garter Stitch = 4-in (10 cm) square

NOTES

- Hat is worked flat and can be knit on straight needles if desired.
- Stitch counts for Large/Extra-Large size will be shown in parentheses.
- For a photo tutorial on how to work I-cord, see page 116.

Body

Using long-tail method and circular needle, CO 60 (64) sts. Do not join.

Rows 1 (WS)–32 (36): Knit.

Decrease Shaping

Row 1: K30 (32), place marker, k30 (32).
Row 2: K1, ssk, knit to 2 sts before marker, ssk, slip marker, k2tog, knit to 3 sts before end, k2tog, k1—56 (60) sts.
Row 3: Knit.
Row 4: Rep row 2—52 (56) sts.
Row 5: Knit.
Row 6: Rep row 2—48 (52) sts.
Row 7: Knit.
Row 8: Rep row 2—44 (48) sts.
Row 9: Knit.

Row 10: Rep row 2—40 (44) sts.
Row 11: Knit.
Row 12: Rep row 2—36 (40) sts.
Row 13: Knit.
Row 14: Rep row 2—32 (36) sts.
Row 15: Knit.
Row 16: Rep row 2—28 (32) sts.
Row 17: Knit.

Finishing

Loosely bind off remaining stitches. Cut yarn, leaving a 6-in (15 cm) tail and draw through last stitch to secure end. Fold hat in half vertically with wrong side facing out. Cut 12-in (30 cm) piece of yarn and use yarn needle to sew together the short edges. Continue sewing along the slanted edge, ending at bottom edge. Weave in yarn tails on inside of hat. Turn hat right-side out.

Using one double-pointed needle, pick up three stitches along the right bottom corner edge. Using second double-pointed needle, knit 50 rows of I-cord. Repeat on left bottom corner edge. Secure ends and hide I-cord tails in the center of I-cord.

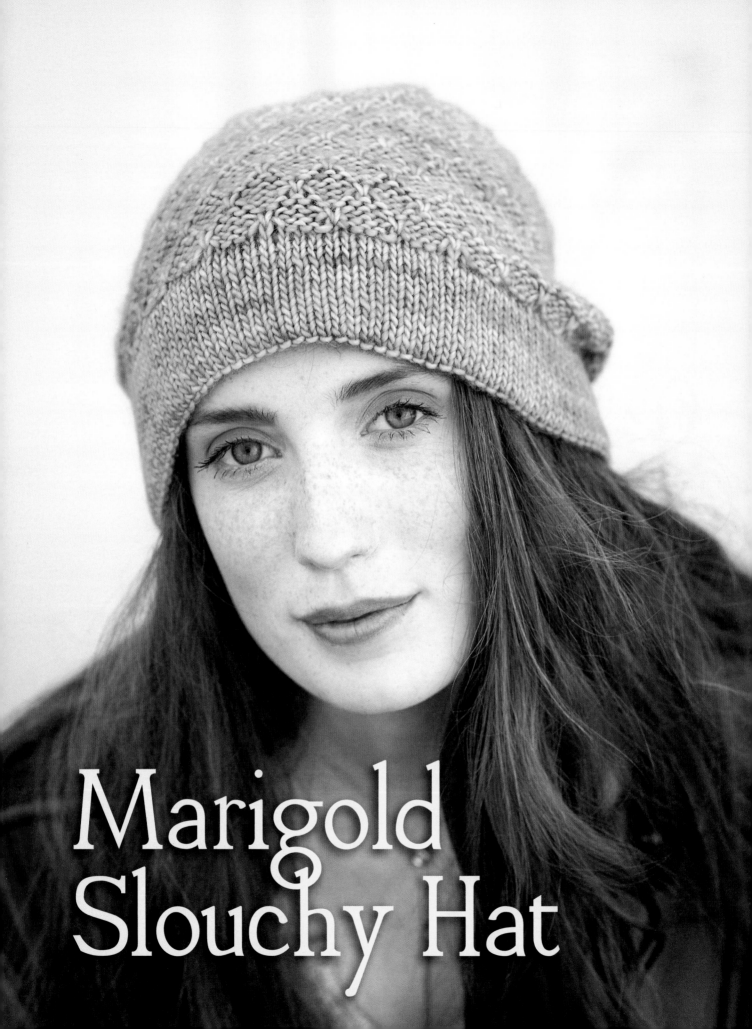

Marigold Slouchy Hat

Elongated stitches decorate a field of reverse stockinette to create this golden slouchy hat. The double brim adds warmth and polish. Choose a smooth single-ply yarn with a delicate drape to make the most of this charming pattern.

FINISHED MEASUREMENTS

Small/Medium:

Circumference at brim band, unstretched: 20 in (51 cm); will fit head circumference of 20 to 22 in (50.5 to 56 cm)

Length from brim edge to crown: 9½ in (24 cm)

Large/Extra-Large:

Circumference at brim band, unstretched: 22 in (56 cm); will fit head circumference of 22 to 24 in (56 to 61 cm)

Length from brim edge to crown: 9½ in (24 cm)

YARN

Small/Medium: 180 yd (165 m) DK weight #3 yarn

Large/Extra-Large: 200 yd (183 m) DK weight #3 yarn; shown knitted in Candlewick, Madelinetosh Tosh Merino DK, 100% merino, 225 yd (206 m) and 3.5 oz (100 g) per skein

NEEDLES AND OTHER MATERIALS

- One 16-in (40.5 cm) circular knitting needle, US 6 (4.25 mm) or size needed to obtain gauge
- US 6 (4.25 mm) set of 5 double-pointed needles or size needed to obtain gauge
- Stitch marker
- Scissors
- Yarn needle

GAUGE

20 sts x 28 rows in Stockinette Stitch = 4-in (10 cm) square

SPECIAL STITCH

Knit 2 below (k2b): Holding the working yarn behind the needles, insert the right needle into the front of the first stitch two rows below the next stitch on the left needle from left to right. Wrap the yarn around the right needle counterclockwise. Pull the yarn through the stitch. Slip the stitch off the left needle.

STITCH PATTERN

Rnds 1–2: Purl.
Rnd 3: *P3, k2b; rep from * around.
Rnds 4–6: Purl.
Rnd 7: P1, *k2b, p3; rep from * around until last 2 sts, p2.
Rnd 8: Purl.

NOTES

- Hat is worked in rounds from bottom edge to crown. Switch from circular needles to double-pointed needles when necessary during crown shaping.
- Stitch counts for Large/Extra-Large size will be shown in parentheses.
- For a photo tutorial on how to knit 2 below, see page 110.

Brim

Using long-tail method and circular needle, CO 96 (104) sts. Place a stitch marker between first and last sts and join in the round, being careful not to twist the cast-on row.
Rnds 1–12: Knit.
Rnd 13: Purl.
Rnds 14–25: Knit.
Fold brim up at purl row to inside of hat. Matching row for row, pick up one stitch from the cast-on row and knit together with the working stitch of the same row, hemming the rows together. Work the entire hat brim hem around in this manner.

Body

Rnds 1–48: Work entire Stitch Pattern 6 times.

Crown Shaping

Rnd 1: *P2tog, p6; rep from * around—84 (91) sts.
Rnd 2: Purl.
Rnd 3: *P2tog, k2b, p3, k2b; rep from * around—72 (78) sts.
Rnd 4: Purl.
Rnd 5: *P2tog, p4; rep from * around—60 (65) sts.
Rnd 6: Purl.
Rnd 7: *P2tog, k2b, p2; rep from * around—48 (52) sts.
Rnd 8: Purl.
Rnd 9: *P2tog, p2; rep from * around—36 (39) sts.
Rnd 10: Purl.
Rnd 11 (size S/M only): *P2tog, p1, p2tog, k2b; rep from * around—24 sts.
Rnd 11 (size L/XL only): *P2tog, p1, p2tog, k2b; rep from * around until last 3 sts, p2tog, p1—(26) sts.
Rnd 12: Purl.
Rnd 13: *P2tog; rep from * around—12 (13) sts.

Finishing

Cut yarn, leaving an 8-in (20.5 cm) tail. Thread yarn needle with end and pick up remaining stitches on knitting needles. Pull tightly to close and secure end. Weave in yarn tails on inside of hat.

Mama Bear
Hooded Cowl

This one-piece hood and cowl is designed to keep the chill out. Super-bulky yarn and large needles make for an ultra-fast project. Optional knitted ears make this knit both fun and functional.

FINISHED MEASUREMENTS

Circumference at bottom neck band, unstretched: 24 in (61 cm); will fit head circumference of 20 to 24 in (50.5 to 61 cm)
Length from neck band edge to crown: 19 in (48 cm)

YARN

150 yd (137 m) super-bulky #6 yarn; shown on page 33 knitted in #640-404 Wood, shown here knitted in #640-146 Fig, Lion Brand Wool-Ease Thick & Quick, 86% acrylic, 10% wool, 4% rayon, 106 yd (97 m) and 6 oz (170 g) per skein

NEEDLES AND OTHER MATERIALS

- One 24-in (61 cm) circular knitting needle, US 15 (10 mm) or size needed to obtain gauge
- US 13 (9 mm) set of 2 double-pointed needles or size needed to obtain gauge
- Stitch marker
- Scissors
- Yarn needle

GAUGE

8 sts x 11 rows in Stockinette Stitch = 4-in (10 cm) square

NOTES

Hood Stitch Pattern:

Row 1: K3, p36, k3.
Row 2: Knit.

NOTES

- This piece is worked from the bottom of the cowl up.
- The cowl section is knit in the round, while the hood section is knit in rows.
- For a photo tutorial on the Kitchener stitch, see page 126.

Ears (Make 2)

Using double-pointed needle, CO 5 sts.
Row 1 (RS): Knit.
Row 2: Kf&b—10 sts.
Rows 3–4: Knit.
Row 5: K1, k2tog, k4, k2tog, k1—8 sts.
Row 6: Knit.
Row 7: K1, k2tog, k2, k2tog, k1—6 sts.
Row 8: Knit.
Row 9: K1, k2tog twice, k1—4 sts.
Row 10: Knit.
Bind off and secure end. Cut yarn leaving an 8-in (20 cm) tail for sewing. Weave in cast-on tails.

Cowl

Using long-tail method and circular needle, CO 48 sts. Place a stitch marker between first and last sts and join in the round, being careful not to twist the cast-on row.
Rnds 1–6: *K1, p1; rep from * around.
Rnds 7–18: Knit.
Rnd 19: *K6, k2tog; rep from * around—42 sts.

Hood

Turn the piece to begin working in the opposite direction.
Rows 1–40: Work entire Hood Stitch Pattern 20 times.
Row 41: Repeat row 1 of Hood Stitch Pattern.

Finishing

Cut yarn, leaving 14-in (36 cm) tail. Fold top row in half with both needle tips pointing to the right and wrong sides of the knitted fabric facing each other. Evenly place 21 stitches on each end of the needle. Thread yarn needle with tail and use the Kitchener stitch to graft the live stitches together from brim to crown peak. Continue until one stitch on each knitting needle remains. Run yarn needle through both and secure end.

Affix ears, with right sides facing forward, to either side of the crown top with the inner ear placement measuring 2 in (5 cm) from crown top center and 4 in (10 cm) from face opening. Thread yarn needle with tail and whipstitch each ear to the hood. Weave in yarn tails on inside of hood.

Baby Bear Hooded Cowl

Worked from the bottom up, this adorable hooded cowl requires little finishing and a nearly seamless join. Hood may be worn up or down and is charming in any color for both boy and girl baby cubs. Garter stitches around the face and ribbing at the cowl base provide gentle details and structure.

FINISHED MEASUREMENTS

Circumference at bottom neck band, unstretched: 20 in (50.5 cm); will fit head circumference of 19 to 22 in (48 to 56 cm)

Length from neck band edge to crown: 15½ in (39 cm)

YARN

110 yd (101 m) super-bulky #6 yarn; shown knitted in #640-123 Oatmeal, Lion Brand Wool-Ease Thick & Quick, 82% acrylic, 10% wool, 8% rayon, 106 yd (97 m) and 6 oz (170 g) per skein

NEEDLES AND OTHER MATERIALS

- One 24-in (61 cm) circular knitting needle, US 15 (10 mm) or size needed to obtain gauge
- US 13 (9 mm) set of 2 double-pointed needles or size needed to obtain gauge
- Stitch marker
- Scissors
- Yarn needle

GAUGE

8 sts x 11 rows in Stockinette Stitch = 4-in (10 cm) square

NOTES

Hood Stitch Pattern:

Row 1: K3, p30, k3.
Row 2: Knit.

NOTES

- This piece is worked from the bottom of the cowl up.
- The cowl section will be knit in the round, while the hood section will be knit in rows.
- For a photo tutorial on the Kitchener stitch, see page 126.

Ears (Make 2)

Using double-pointed needle, CO 5 sts.
Row 1 (RS): Knit.
Row 2: Kf&b of each stitch—10 sts.
Rows 3-4: Knit.
Row 5: K1, k2tog, k4, k2tog, k1—8 sts.
Row 6: Knit.
Row 7: K1, k2tog, k2, k2tog, k1—6 sts.
Row 8: Knit.
Row 9: K1, k2tog twice, k1—4 sts.
Row 10: Knit.
Bind off and secure end. Cut yarn leaving
   an 8-in (20 cm) tail for sewing. Weave in
   cast-on tails.

Cowl

Using long-tail method and circular needle, CO
   42 sts. Place a stitch marker between first and
   last sts and join in the round, being careful
   not to twist the cast-on row.
Rnds 1-6: *K1, p1; rep from * around.
Rnds 7-16: Knit.
Rnd 17: *K5, k2tog; rep from * around—36 sts.

Hood

Turn the piece to begin working in the opposite
   direction.
Rows 1-30: Work entire Hood Stitch
   Pattern 15 times.
Row 31: Repeat row 1 of Hood Stitch Pattern.

Finishing

Cut yarn, leaving 14-in (36 cm) tail. Fold top
   row in half with both needle tips pointing
   to the right and wrong sides of the knitted
   fabric facing each other. Evenly place 18
   stitches on each end of the needle. Thread
   yarn needle with tail and use Kitchener stitch
   to graft the live stitches together from brim
   to crown peak. Continue until one stitch on
   each knitting needle remains. Run yarn needle
   through both and secure end.
Affix ears, with right sides facing forward, to
   either side of the crown top with the inner
   ear placement measuring 2 in (5 cm) from
   crown top center and 4 in (10 cm) from face
   opening. Thread yarn needle with tail and
   whipstitch each ear to the hood. Weave in
   yarn tails on inside of hood.

Conch Beret

*R*ight twists grow out from a ribbed brim and spiral toward a puckered crown. A sturdy plied yarn will provide the best stitch definition. This salmon-colored yarn is flattering against every skin tone.

FINISHED MEASUREMENTS

Circumference at brim band, unstretched: 19 in (48 cm); will fit head circumference of 20 to 23 in (50.5 to 58 cm)

Length from brim edge to crown: 8 in (20 cm)

YARN

155 yd (142 m) worsted weight #4 yarn; shown knitted in #25973 Conch, Knit Picks Wool of the Andes Worsted, 100% Peruvian Highland Wool, 110 yd (101 m) and 1.75 oz (50 g) per ball

NEEDLES AND OTHER MATERIALS

- One 16-in (40.5 cm) circular knitting needle, US 6 (4.0 mm) or size needed to obtain gauge
- US 6 (4.0 mm) set of 5 double-pointed needles or size needed to obtain gauge
- Stitch marker
- Scissors
- Yarn needle

GAUGE

20 sts x 24 rows in Stitch Pattern = 4-in (10 cm) square

SPECIAL STITCHES

Right twist (RT): Insert the right needle into second stitch on the left needle knitwise. Wrap the working yarn around the right needle counterclockwise. Pull the working yarn through the stitch, leaving the stitch on the needle. Insert the right needle into the first stitch on the left needle knitwise. Wrap the working yarn around the right needle counterclockwise. Pull the working yarn through the stitch, sliding both stitches off the left needle.

Make 1 left (M1L) increase: Insert the left needle from front to back into the horizontal strand between the stitches on the right and left needles. Knit the lifted loop through the back.

STITCH PATTERN

Rnd 1: *RT, k3; rep from * around.

Rnd 2: Knit until last st. Slip last st to right-hand needle, remove stitch marker, replace slipped st to left-hand needle, replace marker.

NOTES

- Hat is worked in rounds from bottom edge to crown. Switch from circular needles to double-pointed needles when necessary during crown shaping.
- For photo tutorials on right twist and make 1 left increase, see pages 111 and 120.

Brim

Using long-tail method and circular needle, CO 100 sts. Place a stitch marker between first and last sts and join in the round, being careful not to twist the cast-on row.

Rnds 1–10: *K1, p1; rep from * around.

Rnd 11: *K2, M1L; rep from * around—150 sts.

Rnd 12: Knit.

Rnd 13: *K3, RT; rep from * around.

Rnd 14: Knit.

Rnd 15: K2, RT, *k3, RT*; rep from * around until last st, k1.

Rnd 16: Knit.

Rnd 17: K1, *RT, k3; rep from * around until last 4 sts, RT, k2.

Rnd 18: Knit.

Body

Rnds 1–36: Work entire Stitch Pattern 18 times.

Crown Shaping

Rnd 1: *K2tog, k3; rep from * around—120 sts.

Rnd 2: Knit until last st. Slip last st to right-hand needle, remove stitch marker, replace slipped st to left-hand needle, replace marker.

Rnd 3: *K2tog, k2; rep from * around—90 sts.

Rnd 4: Repeat rnd 2.

Rnd 5: *K2tog, k1; rep from * around—60 sts.

Rnd 6: Repeat rnd 2.

Rnd 7: *K2tog; rep from * around—30 sts.

Finishing

Cut yarn, leaving an 8-in (20.5 cm) tail. Thread yarn needle with end and pick up remaining stitches on knitting needles. Pull tightly to close and secure end. Weave in yarn tails on inside of hat.

Hyacinth Bow Beret

This chunky knitted beret features a faux band detail and oversized bow. Simple decreases create an attractive crown shaping. This combination of gray and blue-toned pink balances this piece as sophisticated and winsome.

FINISHED MEASUREMENTS

Circumference at brim band, unstretched: 17 in (43 cm); will fit head circumference of 20 to 23 in (50.5 cm to 58 cm)

Length from brim edge to crown: 10 in (25 cm)

YARN

MC: 120 yd (110 m) bulky weight #5 yarn; shown knitted in #0033 Slate, Willow Yarns Daily Bulky, 100% super-wash wool, 106 yd (97 m) and 3.5 oz (100 g) per skein

CC: 35 yd (32 m) bulky weight #5 yarn; shown knitted in #0020 Hyacinth, Willow Yarns Daily Bulky, 100% super-wash wool, 106 yd (97 m) and 3.5 oz (100 g) per skein

NEEDLES AND OTHER MATERIALS

- One 16-in (40.5 cm) circular knitting needle, US 10 (6.0 mm) or size needed to obtain gauge
- US 10 (6.0 mm) set of 5 double-pointed needles or size needed to obtain gauge
- Stitch marker
- Scissors
- Yarn needle

GAUGE

15 sts x 19 rows in Stockinette Stitch = 4-in (10 cm) square

SPECIAL STITCHES

Make 1 left (M1L) increase: Insert the left needle from front to back into the horizontal strand between the stitches on the right and left needles. Knit the lifted loop through the back.

Crown Shaping

Rnd 1: *Ssk, k12, k2tog; rep from * around—84 sts.
Rnd 2: Knit.
Rnd 3: *Ssk, k10, k2tog; rep from * around—72 sts.
Rnd 4: Knit.
Rnd 5: *Ssk, k8, k2tog; rep from * around—60 sts.
Rnd 6: Knit.
Rnd 7: *Ssk, k6, k2tog; rep from * around—48 sts.
Rnd 8: Knit.
Rnd 9: *Ssk, k4, k2tog; rep from * around—36 sts.
Rnd 10: Knit.
Rnd 11: *Ssk, k2, k2tog; rep from * around—24 sts.
Rnd 12: Knit.
Rnd 13: *Ssk, k2tog; rep from * around—12 sts.
Rnd 14: Knit.

Finishing

Cut yarn, leaving an 8-in (20.5 cm) tail. Thread yarn needle with end and pick up remaining stitches on knitting needles. Pull tightly to close and secure end. Weave in yarn tails on inside of hat.

Bow

Using long-tail method and two double-pointed needles, CO 12 sts in CC.
Rows 1–80: Knit.
Bind off all sts and secure end. Cut yarn leaving a 15-in (38 cm) tail for sewing. Thread yarn needle with end and sew bind-off edge to cast on edge. Position the bow tube with the seam in the center back. Pinch tube from the top and bottom center to resemble a bow and wrap yarn tail around center pinch several times. Position the bow on the hat along the colorwork rounds. Use remaining tail to sew bow to hat. Sew both bow loops to the hat, sewing through the backs of the bow loops only. Weave in yarn tails on inside of hat.

NOTES
- Hat is worked in rounds from bottom edge to crown. Switch from circular needles to double-pointed needles when necessary during crown shaping.
- Bow is knit separately and sewn on.
- For a photo tutorial on the make 1 left increase, see page 120.

Brim and Body

Using long-tail method and circular needles, CO 64 sts in MC. Place a stitch marker between first and last sts and join in the round, being careful not to twist the cast-on row.
Rnds 1–10: *K2, p2; rep from * around.
Rnds 11–15: *K2 MC, p2 CC; rep from * around.
Rnd 16: *With MC, k2, p2; rep from * around
Rnd 17: Knit.
Rnd 18: *K2, M1L; rep from * around—96 sts.
Rnds 19–36: Knit.

Nubbins Slouchy Hat

Strategically placed raised stitches stud this slightly slouchy hat. Quick decreases produce a gently gathered crown. Choose coordinating neutral tones—or really go for it with contrasting colors.

FINISHED MEASUREMENTS

Circumference at brim band, unstretched: 16 in (41 cm); will fit head circumference of 20 to 23 in (50.5 to 58 cm)

Length from brim edge to crown: 9 in (23 cm)

YARN

MC: 100 yd (91 m) worsted weight #4 yarn; shown knitted in #77009 Flagstone, Patons Classic Wool Worsted, 100% wool, 210 yd (192 m) and 3.5 oz (100 g) per ball

CC: 70 yd (64 m) worsted weight #4 yarn; shown knitted in #77215 Heath Heather, Patons Classic Wool Worsted, 100% wool, 210 yd (192 m) and 3.5 oz (100 g) per skein

NEEDLES AND OTHER MATERIALS

- One 16-in (40.5 cm) circular knitting needle, US 7 (4.5 mm) or size needed to obtain gauge
- US 7 (4.5 mm) set of 5 double-pointed needles or size needed to obtain gauge
- Stitch marker
- Scissors
- Yarn needle

GAUGE

18 sts x 26 rows in Stockinette Stitch = 4-in (10 cm) square

SPECIAL STITCH

Popcorn stitch (Pcs): Holding the working yarn behind the needles, knit into the next stitch, leaving it on the left needle. Holding the working yarn in front of your needles, purl into the same stitch, leaving it on the left needle. Holding the working yarn behind the needles, knit into the same stitch, leaving it on the left needle. Holding the working yarn in front of your needles, purl into the same stitch, slip the stitch off the left needle.

STITCH PATTERN

Rnds 1–3: With CC, knit all sts.
Rnd 4: *Pcs1 MC, k3 CC; rep from * around.
Rnd 5: *With CC, sl3p, k1, pass 3 slipped sts over, k3; rep from * around.
Rnds 6 and 7: With CC, knit all sts.
Rnds 8–10: With MC, knit all sts.
Rnd 11: K2 MC, *Pcs1 CC, k3 MC; rep from * around until last st, k1 MC.
Rnd 12: With MC k2, *sl3p, k1, pass 3 slipped sts over, k3; rep from * around until last st, k1.
Rnds 13 and 14: With MC, knit all sts.

NOTES

- Hat is worked in rounds from bottom edge to crown. Switch from circular needles to double-pointed needles when necessary during crown shaping.
- For a photo tutorial on how to work the popcorn stitch, see page 119.

Brim

Using long-tail method and circular needle, CO 88 sts with MC. Place a stitch marker between first and last sts and join in the round, being careful not to twist the cast-on row.
Rnds 1–12: *K1, p1; rep from * around.
Rnd 13: Purl.

Body

Rnds 1–42: Work entire Stitch Pattern 3 times.

Crown Shaping

Rnd 1: With CC, knit all sts.
Rnd 2: *With CC, k5, sl1k, k2tog, psso; rep from * around—66 sts.
Rnd 3: With CC, knit all sts.

Rnd 4: *Pcs1 MC, with CC k2, sl1k, k2tog, psso; rep from * around—77 sts.
Rnd 5: *With CC, sl3p, k1, pass 3 slipped sts over, k3; rep from * around—44 sts.
Rnd 6: *With CC, k1, sl1k, k2tog, psso; rep from * around—22 sts.
Rnd 7: *With CC, k2tog; rep from * around—11 sts.

Finishing

Cut yarn, leaving an 8-in (20.5 cm) tail. Thread yarn needle with end and pick up remaining stitches on knitting needles. Pull tightly to close and secure end. Weave in yarn tails on inside of hat.

Pine Hill Drive Beret

*F*ew things stick with us quite like the memories of our childhood home. Pine Hill Drive was the street on which I lived when growing up in Vermont. This slightly oversized, stranded colorwork beret pattern is completely charted. A self-striping yarn paired with a solid yarn adds complexity to a deceptively easy project.

FINISHED MEASUREMENTS

Circumference at brim band, unstretched: 20 in (51 cm); will fit head circumference of 21 to 23 in (53 to 58 cm)
Length from brim edge to crown: 8½ in (22 cm)

YARN

MC: 95 yd (87 m) worsted weight #4 yarn; shown knitted in #M-10 Cream, Brown Sheep Company Lamb's Pride Worsted, 85% wool, 15% mohair, 190 yd (173 m) and 4 oz (113 g) per skein

CC: 90 yd (82 m) worsted weight #4 yarn; shown knitted in #26467 Vermont, Knit Picks Chroma Worsted, 70% wool, 30% nylon, 198 yd (181 m) per skein

NEEDLES AND OTHER MATERIALS

- One 16-in (40.5 cm) circular knitting needle, US 3 (3.25 mm)
- One 16-in (40.5 cm) circular knitting needle, US 6 (4 mm) or size needed to obtain gauge
- US 6 (4 mm) set of 5 double-pointed needles or size needed to obtain gauge
- Stitch marker
- Scissors
- Yarn needle

GAUGE

20 sts x 24 rows in Stockinette Stitch using US 6 (4 mm) needles = 4-in (10 cm) square

SPECIAL STITCHES

Slip 2 together knitwise, knit 1, pass slipped stitches over decrease (s2kp2): Use the tip of your right needle to slip the first two stitches together off the left needle knitwise. Knit the next stitch. Use your left needle to pass the slipped stitches over the knit stitch and off the right needle.

Make 1 left (M1L) increase: Insert the left needle from front to back into the horizontal strand between the stitches on the right and left needles. Knit the lifted loop through the back.

NOTES

- Hat is worked in rounds from bottom edge to crown. Switch from circular needles to double-pointed needles when necessary during crown shaping.
- Color charts are read from bottom to top and from right to left.
- For photo tutorials on the make 1 left increase and the slip 2 together knitwise, knit 1, pass slipped stitches over decrease, see pages 120 and 124.

Brim

Using long-tail method and US 3 (3.25 mm) circular needle, CO 100 sts with MC. Place a stitch marker between first and last sts and join in the round, being careful not to twist the cast-on row.

Rnd 1: Knit.
Rnds 2–8: *K1 MC, p1 CC; rep from * around.
Rnd 9: With MC, knit.
Rnd 10: *K5, M1L; rep from * around—120 sts.

Body

Switch to US 6 (4 mm) circular needle.
Rnds 1–37: Working in Stockinette Stitch, follow the entire color chart 1 for 37 rounds.

Crown Shaping

Follow color chart 2 and instructions below.
Rnd 1: *S2kp2, k17; rep from * around—108 sts.
Rnd 2: Knit.
Rnd 3: *S2kp2, k15; rep from * around—96 sts.
Rnd 4: Knit.
Rnd 5: *S2kp2, k13; rep from * around—84 sts.
Rnd 6: Knit.

Chart 1

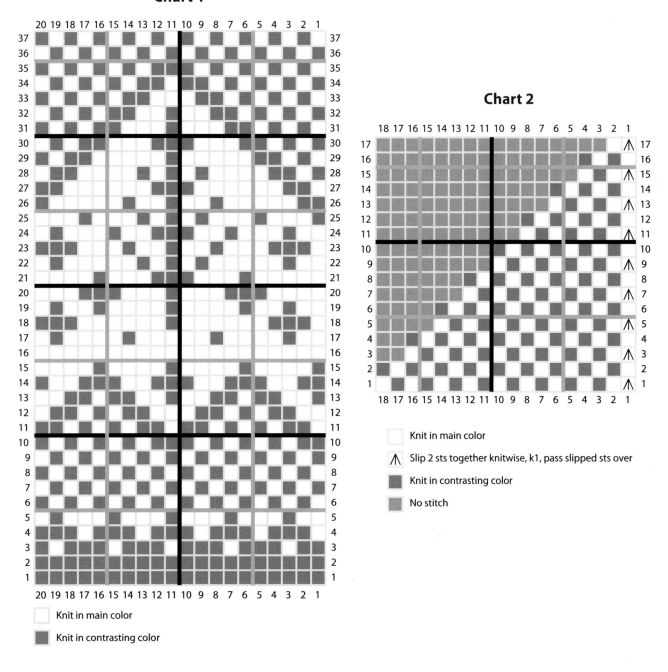

Knit in main color

Knit in contrasting color

Chart 2

Knit in main color

⋀ Slip 2 sts together knitwise, k1, pass slipped sts over

Knit in contrasting color

No stitch

Rnd 7: *S2kp2, k11; rep from * around—72 sts.
Rnd 8: Knit.
Rnd 9: *S2kp2, k9; rep from * around—60 sts.
Rnd 10: Knit.
Rnd 11: *S2kp2, k7; rep from * around—48 sts.
Rnd 12: Knit.
Rnd 13: *S2kp2, k5; rep from * around—36 sts.
Rnd 14: Knit.
Rnd 15: *S2kp2, k3; rep from * around—24 sts.
Rnd 16: Knit.
Rnd 17: *S2kp2, k1; rep from * around—12 sts.

Finishing

Cut yarn, leaving an 8-in (20.5 cm) tail. Thread yarn needle with end and pick up remaining stitches on knitting needles. Pull tightly to close and secure end. Weave in yarn tails on inside of hat. Wet block hat and form over a 10-inch disc of cardboard or a dinner plate to dry.

Ombre Marled Pixie Hood

This multicolored pixie hood is a beautiful example of marling, a process of knitting with two different-colored yarns held together. Marling is a superb way of using up remnant yarns. The remnants used to make this hat were leftovers from a Fair Isle pattern in my first book, *Knitted Beanies and Slouchy Hats*.

FINISHED MEASUREMENTS

Length at brim band, unstretched: 19 in (48 cm); will fit head circumference of 21 to 23 in (53 to 58 cm)

Depth from brim edge to crown point: 11 in (28 cm)

YARN

Color A: 70 yd (64 m) worsted weight #4 yarn; shown knitted in #184 Aloe, Lion Brand Yarn Wool-Ease Worsted Weight, 80% acrylic, 20% wool, 197 yd (180 m) and 3 oz (85 g) per skein

Color B: 70 yd (64 m) worsted weight #4 yarn; shown knitted in #177 Loden, Lion Brand Yarn Wool-Ease Worsted Weight, 80% acrylic, 20% wool, 197 yd (180 m) and 3 oz (85 g) per skein

Color C: 70 yd (64 m) worsted weight #4 yarn; shown knitted in #123 Seaspray, Lion Brand Yarn Wool-Ease Worsted Weight, 80% acrylic, 20% wool, 197 yd (180 m) and 3 oz (85 g) per skein

Color D: 70 yd (64 m) worsted weight #4 yarn; shown knitted in #191 Violet, Lion Brand Yarn Wool-Ease Worsted Weight, 80% acrylic, 20% wool, 197 yd (180 m) and 3 oz (85 g) per skein

NEEDLES AND OTHER MATERIALS

- One 24-in (61 cm) circular knitting needle, US 11 (8.0 mm) or size needed to obtain gauge
- Scissors
- Yarn needle

GAUGE

11 sts x 16 rows in Stockinette Stitch = 4-in (10 cm) square

STITCH PATTERN

Row 1 (RS): Knit.
Row 2: K4, p52, k4.

Body

Rows 1 (RS)–32: Work entire Stitch Pattern 16 times. Change yarn to colors B and C at row 10. Change yarn to colors C and D at row 22.

Row 33: Repeat row 1 of Stitch Pattern.

Row 34: Change yarn colors to D and A. P2tog twice, p to last 4 sts, p2tog twice—56 sts.

Row 35: K2tog twice, k to last 4 sts, k2tog twice—52 sts.

Row 36: Repeat row 34—48 sts.

Row 37: Repeat row 35—44 sts.

Row 38: Repeat row 34—40 sts.

Row 39: Repeat row 35—36 sts.

Row 40: Repeat row 34—32 sts.

Row 41: Bind off 4 sts, k28—28 sts.

Row 42: Bind off 4 sts, p24—24 sts.

Row 43: Bind off 4 sts, k20—20 sts.

Row 44: Bind off 4 sts, p16—16 sts.

Finishing

Bind off remaining stitches. Cut yarn, leaving a 6-in (15 cm) tail and draw through last stitch to secure end. Fold hat in half vertically with wrong side facing out. Cut 16-in (41 cm) piece of yarn and use yarn needle to sew together the back seam. Weave in yarn tails on inside of hat. Turn hat right-side out.

To make a tassel, cut a 7-in (18 cm) long piece of cardboard. Holding one strand of all four colors of yarn together, wrap working yarn around the cardboard 10 or more times, depending on how thick you would like the tassel to be, and cut the end of yarn on the same side where the wrapping began. Holding the opposite end of the bundle, slide scissors between the cardboard and the yarn, and cut the remaining strands of yarn to free the tassel. Part a space in the knitted fabric of one of the corners of the hood; feed the uncut side of the tassel through the knitting to form a loop. Feed the cut ends through the loop and tighten. Repeat these steps for the second tassel. Trim ends as needed.

NOTES

- Hat is worked flat in rows from bottom edge to point edge.
- Two strands of yarn will be held together throughout the project.
- For a photo tutorial on how to make a tassel, see page 129.

Brim

Using long-tail method, CO 60 sts with colors A and B. Do not join.

Rows 1–3: Knit.

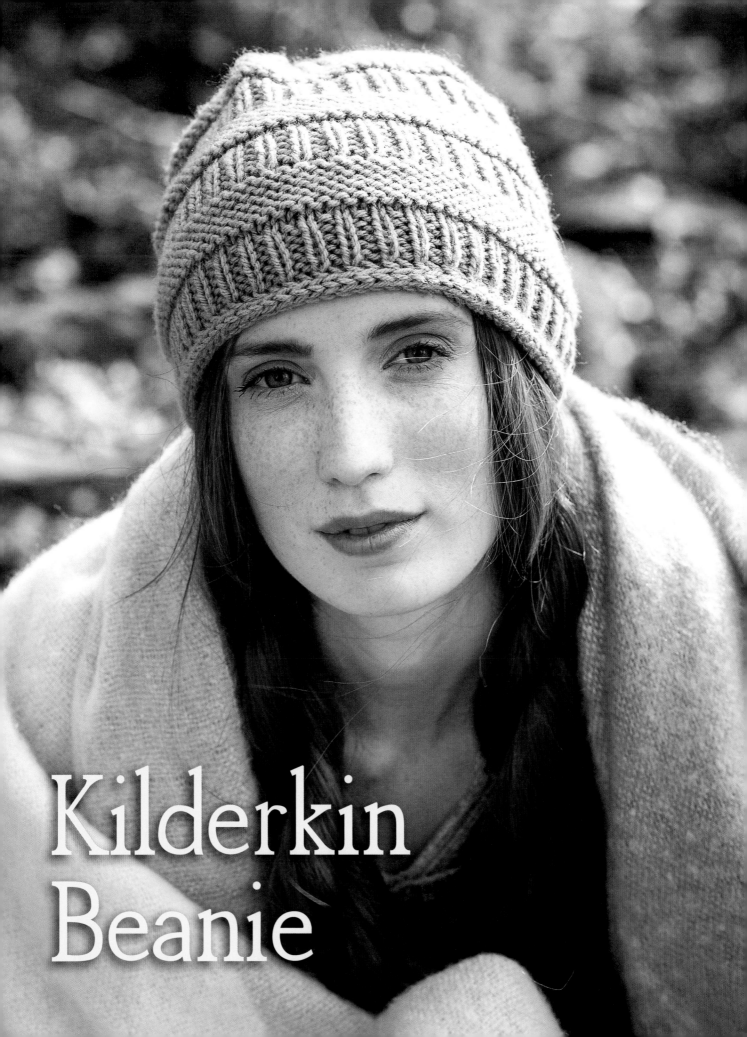

Kilderkin
Beanie

With its strong lines, this handsome beanie is ideal for every member of the family. Purl ridges mimic an I-cord brim, separated by columns of ribbing. Resembling a small barrel, this clever pattern comes in three sizes.

FINISHED MEASUREMENTS

Small:

Circumference at brim band, unstretched: 16 in (41 cm); will fit head circumference of 20 to 21 in (51 to 53 cm)

Length from brim edge to crown: 8 in (20 cm)

Medium:

Circumference at brim band, unstretched: 17 in (43 cm); will fit head circumference of 21 to 22 in (53 to 56 cm)

Length from brim edge to crown: 8 in (20 cm)

Large:

Circumference at brim band, unstretched: 18 in (46 cm); will fit head circumference of 22 to 23 in (56 to 58 cm)

Length from brim edge to crown: 8 in (20 cm)

YARN

Small: 101 yd (92 m) worsted weight #4 yarn; shown knitted in #108920 Soft Taupe, Loops & Threads Impeccable, 100% acrylic, 268 yd (245 m) and 4.5 oz (127.5 g) per skein

Medium: 111 yd (101 m) worsted weight #4 yarn

Large: 121 yd (111 m) worsted weight #4 yarn

NEEDLES AND OTHER MATERIALS

- One 16-in (40.5 cm) circular knitting needle, US 8 (5.0 mm) or size needed to obtain gauge
- US 8 (5.0 mm) set of 5 double-pointed needles or size needed to obtain gauge
- Stitch marker
- Scissors
- Yarn needle

GAUGE

16 sts x 20 rows in Reverse Stockinette Stitch = 4-in (10 cm) square

STITCH PATTERN

Rnd 1: Knit.
Rnds 2–6: *K1, p1; rep from * around.
Rnd 7: Knit.
Rnds 8–12: Purl.

NOTES

- Hat begins with an I-cord brim. Hat is then worked in rounds from brim edge to crown. Switch from circular needles to double-pointed needles when necessary during crown shaping.
- Stitch counts for Medium and Large sizes will be shown in parentheses.
- For a photo tutorial on how to work I-cord, see page 116.

Body

Using long-tail method and two double-pointed needles, CO 4 sts. Knit 79 (83, 87) rows of I-cord. Bind off 3 stitches, leaving one loop on the right needle, transfer loop to circular needle and pick up 79 (83, 87) stitches from the I-cord. Place a stitch marker between first and last sts and join in the round—80 (84, 88) sts.

Rnds 1–36: Work entire Stitch Pattern 3 times.

Crown Shaping

Rnd 1: Knit.
Rnds 2–6: *K1, p1; rep from * around.
Rnd 7: Knit.
Rnd 8: *P2, p2tog; rep from * around—60 (63, 66) sts.
Rnd 9: Purl.
Rnd 10: *P1, p2tog; rep from * around—40 (42, 44) sts.
Rnd 11: Purl.
Rnd 12: *P2tog; rep from * around—20 (21, 22) sts.

Finishing

Cut yarn, leaving an 8-in (20.5 cm) tail. Thread yarn needle with end and pick up remaining stitches on knitting needles. Pull tightly to close and secure end. Use cast-on tail to sew together I-cord cast-on ends. Weave in yarn tails on inside of hat.

Driftwood Wrap Hood

This infinity-style hooded wrap is the quintessential accessory for frigid weather. Made with a snuggly soft bouclé yarn, this hood may be worn bundled around the neck or hanging free. Supersized needles make quick work of this project.

FINISHED MEASUREMENTS
Circumference, unstretched: 76 in (193 cm); will fit head circumference of 20 to 24 in (50.5 to 61 cm)
Width from cast-on to bind-off edge: 8½ in (22 cm)
Hood length along back seam: 12 in (30 cm)

YARN
170 yd (155 m) super-bulky weight #6 yarn; shown knitted in #133284 Driftwood, Loops & Threads Country Loom, 100% acrylic, 104 yd (95 m) and 4.94 oz (140 g) per skein

NEEDLES AND OTHER MATERIALS
- One 36-in (91 cm) circular knitting needle, US 17 (12.5 mm) or size needed to obtain gauge
- Stitch marker
- Scissors
- Yarn needle

GAUGE
6 sts x 12 rows in pattern = 4-in (10 cm) square

NOTES
- Hood is worked in rounds from cast-on edge to bind-off edge.

Hat

Using long-tail method and circular needle,
    CO 110 sts. Place a stitch marker between
    first and last sts and join in the round, being
    careful not to twist the cast-on row.

Rnds 1–4: Purl.

Rnds 5–8: Knit.

Rnds 9–12: Purl.

Rnds 13–16: Knit.

Rnds 17–20: Purl.

Rnds 21–24: Knit.

Rnds 25–28: Purl.

Finishing

Bind off all stitches loosely. Cut yarn, leaving
    a 20-in (51 cm) tail. Turn knitted circle inside
    out and lay flat with right sides facing each
    other and tail end to far left. Thread yarn
    needle with tail end. Use tail to sew together
    the two bound-off edges on the left for 12 in
    (30 cm). Secure tail end and weave in yarn
    tails on inside of hood and turn right-side out.

Latvian Lampreys Hat

Serpentine cables flow effortlessly from a floor of Latvian braid, building a thick and thermal fabric. Latvian braids are typically found along cuffs of mittens and sweaters, but they also make a tidy brim. Manage the yarn carefully to avoid tangles.

FINISHED MEASUREMENTS

Small/Medium:

Circumference at brim band, unstretched: 18 in (46 cm); will fit head circumference of 20 to 21 in (50.5 to 53 cm)

Length from brim edge to crown: 8¼ in (21 cm)

Large/Extra-Large:

Circumference at brim band, unstretched: 20 in (51 cm); will fit head circumference of 22 to 23 in (56 to 58 cm)

Length from brim edge to crown: 8¼ in (21 cm)

YARN

Small/Medium:

MC: 70 yd (64 m) bulky weight #5 yarn
CC: 65 yd (59 m) bulky weight #5 yarn

Large/Extra-Large:

MC: 85 yd (78 m) bulky weight #5 yarn; shown knitted in #0045 Cana Lilly, Willow Yarns Daily Bulky, 100% super-wash wool, 106 yd (97 m) and 3.5 oz (100 g) per skein

CC: 80 yd (73 m) bulky weight #5 yarn; shown knitted in #0015 Turquoise, Willow Yarns Daily Bulky, 100% super-wash wool, 106 yd (97 m) and 3.5 oz (100 g) per skein

NEEDLES AND OTHER MATERIALS

- One 16-in (40.5 cm) circular knitting needle, US 9 (5.5 mm) or size needed to obtain gauge
- One 16-in (40.5 cm) circular knitting needle, US 11 (7.0 mm)
- US 11 (7.0 mm) set of 5 double-pointed needles or size needed to obtain gauge
- Stitch marker
- Cable needle
- Scissors
- Yarn needle

GAUGE

16 sts x 20 rows in Stockinette Stitch using larger needle (US 11 or size needed to obtain gauge) = 4-in (10 cm) square

SPECIAL STITCHES

4/4 right cross (4/4 RC): Slip next 4 sts to cable needle, hold cable needle to back of work, knit 4 sts from main needle, knit 4 sts from cable needle.

4/4 left cross (4/4 LC): Slip next 4 sts to cable needle, hold cable needle to front of work, knit 4 sts from main needle, knit 4 sts from cable needle.

Make 1 left (M1L) increase: Insert the left needle from front to back into the horizontal strand between the stitches on the right and left needles. Knit the lifted loop through the back.

STITCH PATTERN

Rnds 1–3: *K2 MC, k2 CC; rep from * around.
Rnd 4: *(K2 MC, k2 CC) twice, 4/4RC; rep from * around.
Rnds 5–7: *K2 MC, k2 CC; rep from * around.
Rnd 8: *4/4LC, (k2 MC, k2 CC) twice; rep from * around.

NOTES

- Hat is worked in rounds from bottom edge to crown. Switch from circular needles to double-pointed needles when necessary during crown shaping.
- Work cable stitches in the color that presents on the left needle. The main color will always be knit into main color stitches, contrasting color will always be knit into contrasting color stitches.
- For photo tutorials on working two-color cast-on method, 4/4 left cross, 4/4 right cross, and make 1 left increase, see pages 103, 114, 115, and 120.

Latvian Braid Brim

Using two-color cast-on method and smaller
  circular needles, CO 64 sts. Place a stitch
  marker between first and last sts and join
  in the round, being careful not to twist the
  cast-on row.

Rnd 1: *K1 MC, k1 CC; rep from * around.

Rnd 2: P1 MC, *cross CC over MC to the left, p1
  CC, cross MC over CC to the left, p1 MC; rep
  from * around until the last st, cross CC over
  MC to the left, p1 CC.

Rnd 3: P1 MC, *cross CC under MC from the
  right, p1 CC, cross MC under CC from the
  right, p1 MC; rep from * around until the last
  st, cross CC under MC from the right, p1 CC.

Rnd 4: Change to larger needles. Knit MC.

Rnd 5 (S/M size only): *K2, M1L; rep from *
  around—96 sts.

Rnd 5 (L/XL size only): *K1, M1L; rep from *
  around—128 sts.

Both sizes:

Rnd 6: Knit.

Body

Rnds 1–24: Work entire Stitch Pattern 3 times.

Crown Shaping

Rnd 1: *K2 MC, k2 CC; rep from * around.

Rnd 2: *K2 MC, k2tog CC; rep from *
  around—72 (96) sts.

Rnd 3: *K2 MC, k1 CC; rep from * around.

Rnd 4: *K2tog MC, k1 CC; rep from *
  around—48 (64) sts.

Rnd 5: *K1 MC, k1 CC; rep from * around.

Rnd 6: *K2tog CC; rep from *
  around—24 (32) sts.

Rnd 7: *K2tog CC; rep from *
  around—12 (16) sts.

Finishing

Cut yarns, leaving an 8-in (20.5 cm) tail.
  Thread yarn needle with CC end and pick up
  remaining stitches on knitting needles. Pull
  tightly to close and secure end. Weave in yarn
  tails on inside of hat.

Parquet
Slouchy Beanie

This graphic basket-weave design is brought to life in a soft peppery red yarn. The casual ease and comfortable slouch of this beanie is a winner with both gents and gals. As quickly as it knits up, you can make one for everyone on your list!

FINISHED MEASUREMENTS
Circumference at brim band, unstretched: 18 in (46 cm); will fit head circumference of 20 to 23 in (50.5 to 58 cm)
Length from brim edge to crown: 9 ½ in (24 cm)

YARN
128 yd (117 m) bulky weight #5 yarn; shown knitted in #0003 Brick, Willow Yarns Daily Bulky, 100% super-wash wool, 106 yd (97 m) and 3.5 oz (100 g) per skein

NEEDLES AND OTHER MATERIALS
- One 16-in (40.5 cm) circular knitting needle, US 10 (6.0 mm) or size needed to obtain gauge
- US 10 (6.0 mm) set of 5 double-pointed needles or size needed to obtain gauge
- Stitch marker
- Scissors
- Yarn needle

GAUGE
12 sts x 18 rows in Stockinette Stitch = 4-in (10 cm) square

SPECIAL STITCHES
Make 1 left (M1L) increase: Insert the left needle from front to back into the horizontal strand between the stitches on the right and left needles. Knit the lifted loop through the back.

NOTES
- Hat is worked in rounds from bottom edge to crown. Switch from circular needles to double-pointed needles when necessary during crown shaping.
- For a photo tutorial on the make 1 left increase, see page 120.

Brim

Using long-tail method and circular needles, CO 60 sts. Place a stitch marker between first and last sts and join in the round, being careful not to twist the cast-on row.

Rnds 1–8: Knit.
Rnds 9–10: Purl.
Rnd 11: *K5, M1L; rep from * around—72 sts.
Rnd 12: Knit.

Body

Rnd 1: (K2, p2) twice, *k12, p2, k2, p2; rep from * around until the last 10 sts, k10.
Rnd 2: Repeat rnd 1.
Rnd 3: *(K2, p2) twice, k2, p8; rep from * around.
Rnd 4: Repeat rnd 3.
Rnds 5–6: Repeat rnd 1.
Rnds 7–8: Repeat rnd 3.
Rnds 9–10: Repeat rnd 1.
Rnd 11: K11, p2, k2, p2, *k12, p2, k2, p2; rep from * around until the last st, k1.

Rnd 12: Repeat rnd 11.
Rnd 13: K1, p8, *(k2, p2) twice, k2, p8; rep from * around until the last 9 sts, (k2, p2) twice, k1.
Rnd 14: Repeat rnd 13.
Rnds 15–16: Repeat rnd 11.
Rnds 17–18: Repeat rnd 13.
Rnds 19–20: Repeat rnd 11.
Rnds 21–30: Repeat rnds 1–10.
Rnds 31–40: Repeat rnds 11–20.

Crown Shaping

Rnds 1–4: *K2, p2; rep from * around.
Rnd 5: *K2, p2tog; rep from * around—54 sts.
Rnd 6: *K2tog, p1; rep from * around—36 sts.
Rnd 7: *K2tog; rep from * around—18 sts.

Finishing

Cut yarn, leaving an 8-in (20.5 cm) tail. Thread yarn needle with end and pick up remaining stitches on knitting needles. Pull tightly to close and secure end. Weave in yarn tails on inside of hat.

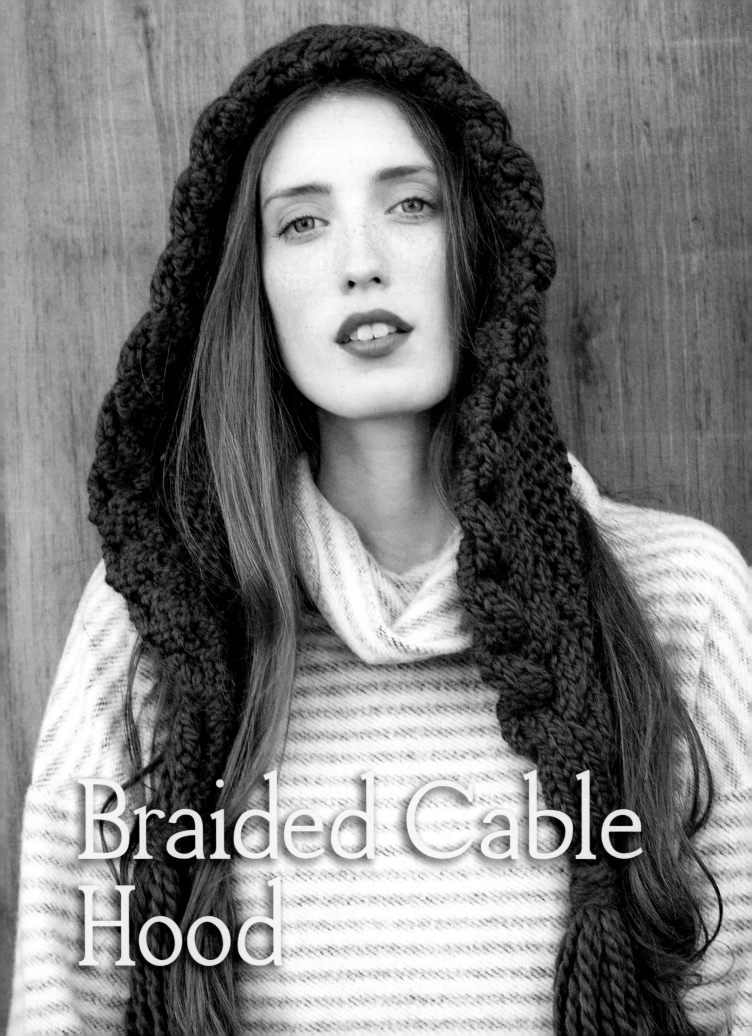

Braided Cable
Hood

Bonnet-style hoods are a chic and trendy accessory and an effective way of avoiding hat hair. This romantic hood features a chunky cable brim flanked by oversized tassels. The deep, rich wine-colored yarn gives the perfect pop of color on a snowy day.

FINISHED MEASUREMENTS

Length of hood cable including fringe: 56 in (142 cm)

Width of cable: 2 in (5 cm)

Width from cable edge to back of crown: 9 in (23 cm); will fit head circumference of 20 to 24 in (50.5 to 61 cm)

YARN

150 yd (137 m) super-bulky #6 yarn; shown knitted in #2430 Merlot, Loops & Threads Cozy Wool Yarn, 50% acrylic, 50% wool, 90 yd (82 m) and 4.5 oz (127.5 g) per skein

NEEDLES AND OTHER MATERIALS

- One 24-in (61 cm) circular knitting needle, US 13 (9.0 mm) or size needed to obtain gauge
- US 13 (9 mm) set of 2 double-pointed needles or size needed to obtain gauge
- Cable needle
- Stitch marker
- Scissors
- Yarn needle

GAUGE

9 sts x 18 rows in Garter Stitch = 4-in (10 cm) square

SPECIAL STITCHES

4/4 right cross (4/4 RC): Slip next 4 sts to cable needle, hold cable needle to back of work, knit 4 sts from main needle, knit 4 sts from cable needle.

4/4 left cross (4/4 LC): Slip next 4 sts to cable needle, hold cable needle to front of work, knit 4 sts from main needle, knit 4 sts from cable needle.

Knit front and back increase (kfb): Knit into the next stitch, leaving it on the left needle. Bring the tip of the right needle around to the back of the stitch and knit into the back loop of the same stitch. Slip the stitches off the left needle.

Make 1 left (M1L) increase: Insert the left needle from front to back into the horizontal strand between the stitches on the right and left needles. Knit the lifted loop through the back.

STITCH PATTERN

Braided Cable:

Row 1: Knit.
Row 2: Purl.
Row 3: 4/4LC, k4.
Row 4: Purl.
Row 5: K4, 4/4RC.
Row 6: Purl.

NOTES

- Hood begins by knitting a cable stitch band. Stitches are then picked up along the band edge.
- Body is knit flat, crown is knit in the round. Switch from circular needles to double-pointed needles when necessary during crown shaping.
- For photo tutorials on working 4/4 left cross, 4/4 right cross, knit front and back increase, make 1 left increase, and making tassels, see pages 114, 115, 120, and 129.

Braided Cable

Using long-tail method and double-pointed needles, CO 2 sts.

Row 1: Purl.
Row 2: Kfb twice—4 sts.
Row 3: Purl.
Row 4: K1, M1L, k2, M1L, k1—6 sts.
Row 5: Purl.
Row 6: K1, M1L, k4, M1L, k1—8 sts.
Row 7: Purl.
Row 8: K1, M1L, k6, M1L, k1—10 sts.

Row 9: Purl.
Row 10: K1, M1L, k8, M1L, k1—12 sts.
Row 11: Purl.
Rows 12–143: Work entire Braided Cable Stitch Pattern 22 times.
Rows 144–147: Work rows 1–4 of Braided Cable Stitch Pattern.
Row 148: K1, k2tog, k6, k2tog, k1—10 sts.
Row 149: Purl.
Row 150: K1, k2tog, k4, k2tog, k1—8 sts.
Row 151: Purl.
Row 152: K1, k2tog, k2, k2tog, k1—6 sts.
Row 153: Purl.
Row 154: K1, k2tog twice, k1—4 sts.
Row 155: Purl.
Row 156: K2tog twice—2 sts.
Bind off.

Hood

Using long-tail method and circular needle, pick up and knit 68 stitches evenly along cable edge.
Row 1: Knit.
Row 2: K1, k2tog, k1, k2tog, k56, k2tog, k1, k2tog, k1—64 sts.
Row 3: Knit.
Row 4: K1, k2tog, k1, k2tog, k52, k2tog, k1, k2tog, k1—60 sts.
Row 5: Knit.
Row 6: K1, k2tog, k1, k2tog, k48, k2tog, k1, k2tog, k1—56 sts.
Row 7: Knit.
Row 8: K1, k2tog, k1, k2tog, k44, k2tog, k1, k2tog, k1—52 sts.
Row 9: Knit.
Row 10: K1, k2tog, k1, k2tog, k40, k2tog, k1, k2tog, k1—48 sts.
Row 11: Knit.
Row 12: K1, k2tog, k1, k2tog, k36, k2tog, k1, k2tog, k1—44 sts.
Row 13: Knit.
Row 14: K1, k2tog, k1, k2tog, k32, k2tog, k1, k2tog, k1—40 sts.
Row 15–22: Knit.
Place a stitch marker between first and last sts and join in the round, being careful not to twist the cast-on row.
Rnd 1: Purl.
Rnd 2: *K3, k2tog; repeat from * around—32 sts.
Rnd 3: Purl.
Rnd 4: *K2, k2tog; repeat from * around—24 sts.

Rnd 5: Purl.
Rnd 6: *K1, k2tog; repeat from * around—16 sts.
Rnd 7: Purl.
Rnd 8: *K2tog; repeat from * around—8 sts.

Finishing

Cut yarn, leaving an 8-in (20.5 cm) tail. Thread yarn needle with end and pick up remaining stitches on knitting needles. Pull tightly to close and secure end. Weave in yarn tails on inside of hat.

To make a tassel, cut a 7-in-long (18 cm) piece of cardboard. Wrap yarn around the cardboard 20 times; cut the end of working yarn on the same side where the wrapping began. Holding the opposite end of the bundle, slide scissors between the cardboard and the yarn and cut the remaining strands of yarn to free the tassel. Part a space in the knitted fabric of one of the ends of the hood cable, feed the uncut side of the tassel through the knitting to form a loop. Feed the cut ends through the loop and tighten. Repeat these steps for the second tassel. Trim ends as needed.

Bougainvillea
Beret

A rush of saturated pinks and mauves speaks of exotic promise, while thorny vines meander from a thick garter brim with a thoughtful button-flap detail. This super-bulky beret redefines lace knitting. A handmade wooden button makes a splendid finishing touch.

FINISHED MEASUREMENTS

Circumference at brim band, unstretched: 19 in (48 cm); will fit head circumference of 20 to 23 in (50.5 to 58 cm)
Length from brim edge to crown: 9 in (23 cm)

YARN

85 yd (78 m) super-bulky weight #6 yarn; shown knitted in #640-525 Wild Strawberry, Lion Brand Wool-Ease Thick & Quick, 80% acrylic, 20% wool, 87 yd (80 m) and 6 oz (170 g) per skein

NEEDLES AND OTHER MATERIALS

- One 16-in (40.5 cm) circular knitting needle, US 11 (8.0 mm)
- One 16-in (40.5 cm) circular knitting needle, US 13 (9.0 mm) or size needed to obtain gauge
- US 13 (9.0 mm) set of 5 double-pointed needles or size needed to obtain gauge
- Stitch marker
- Scissors
- Yarn needle
- One 1¼ in (3 cm) button

GAUGE

9 sts x 12 rows in Stitch Pattern using larger needles (US 13 [9.0 mm] or size needed to obtain gauge) = 4-in (10 cm) square

SPECIAL STITCHES

Make 1 left (M1L) increase: Insert the left needle from front to back into the horizontal strand between the stitches on the right and left needles. Knit the lifted loop through the back.

Brim

Using long-tail method and US 11 (8.0 mm) circular needle, CO 49 sts. Do not join.

Rows 1–3: Knit.

Row 4: Knit until last 4 sts, bind off 1, k3—48 sts.

Row 5: K4, yo, k44—49 sts.

Row 6–8: Knit.

Row 9: Bind off 7, p41—42 sts.

Row 10: Using US 13 (9.0 mm) circular needle, *k3, M1L; repeat from * —56 sts.

Body

Place a stitch marker between first and last sts and join in the round, being careful not to twist the cast-on row.

Rnd 1: Knit.

Rnds 2–17: Work entire Stitch Pattern 4 times.

Crown Shaping

Rnd 1: *K2tog, k3, ssk, k1; repeat from * —42 sts.

Rnd 2: Knit.

Rnd 3: *Sl1k, k2tog, psso, k3; repeat from * —28 sts.

Rnd 4: Knit.

Rnd 5: *K2tog, ssk; repeat from * —14 sts.

Rnd 6: *K2tog; repeat from * —7 sts.

Finishing

Cut yarn, leaving an 8-in (20.5 cm) tail. Thread yarn needle with end and pick up remaining stitches on knitting needles. Pull tightly to close and secure end. Weave in yarn tails on inside of hat.

Sew button to left side of brim, fold right side brim overlap over button and thread button through buttonhole.

STITCH PATTERN

Rnd 1: *K2tog, yo, k3, yo, ssk, k1; rep from * around.

Rnd 2: Knit.

Rnd 3: *Yo, sl1k, k2tog, psso, yo, k5; rep from * around.

Rnd 4: Knit.

NOTES

- Hat brim is worked flat without joining, then joined in the round for crown. Switch from circular needles to double-pointed needles when necessary during crown shaping.
- For a photo tutorial on the make 1 left increase, see page 120.

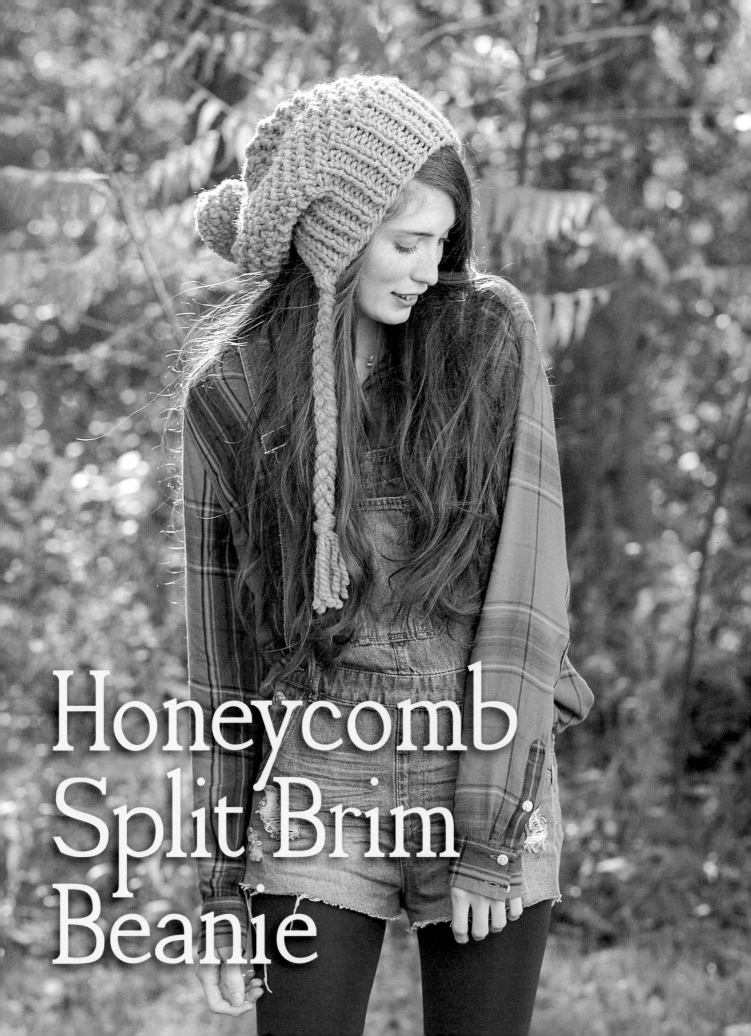

Honeycomb Split Brim Beanie

An offset brioche stitch produces this highly textured fabric, reminiscent of honeycomb. The deep split brim is defined by a pair of youthful braids, and the crown is adorned with a large pom-pom. The rhythmic grace of this stitch pattern is uncomplicated and almost therapeutic to knit.

FINISHED MEASUREMENTS

Circumference at brim band, unstretched: 14 in (36 cm); will fit head circumference of 20 to 23 in (50.5 to 58 cm)

Length from brim edge to crown: 10 in (25 cm)

YARN

140 yd (128 m) super-bulky #6 yarn; shown knitted in #2610 Goldenrod, Loops & Threads Cozy Wool Yarn, 50% acrylic, 50% wool, 90 yd (82 m), and 4.5 oz (127.5 g) per skein

NEEDLES AND OTHER MATERIALS

- One 16-in (40.5 cm) circular knitting needle, US 13 (9.0 mm) or size needed to obtain gauge
- US 13 (9 mm) set of 2 double-pointed needles or size needed to obtain gauge
- Stitch marker
- Scissors
- Yarn needle

GAUGE

8 sts x 10 rows in Stitch Pattern = 4-in (10 cm) square

SPECIAL STITCH

Knit 1 below (k1b): Holding the working yarn behind the needles, insert the right needle into the front of the first stitch directly below the next stitch on the left needle from left to right. Wrap the yarn around the right needle counterclockwise. Pull the yarn though the stitch. Slip the stitch off the left needle.

STITCH PATTERN

Rnd 1: Purl.
Rnd 2: *K1, k1b; repeat from * around.
Rnd 3: Purl.
Rnd 4: *K1b, k1; repeat from * around.

NOTES

- Hat brim is worked flat without joining. Body of hat and crown shaping is knit in the round. Switch from circular needle to double-pointed needles when necessary during crown shaping.
- For photo tutorials on how to work knit 1 below and how to make pom-poms, see pages 110 and 128.

Brim

Using long-tail method and circular needle, CO 41 sts. Do not join.

Row 1 (WS): *K1, p1; repeat from * until last st, k1.

Row 2: *P1, k1; repeat from * until last st, p1.

Rows 3–10: Repeat rows 1 and 2 four times.

Row 11: *K1, p1; repeat from * until last st, k1.

Row 12: *P1, k1; rep from * to last st, join in the round by knitting together the last stitch of this row with the first stitch of the next row and place marker—40 sts.

Body

Rnds 1–28: Work entire Stitch Pattern 7 times.

Rnds 29–30: Work rnds 1 and 2 of Stitch Pattern.

Crown Shaping

Rnd 1: *P3, p2tog; repeat from * around—32 sts.

Rnd 2: *K1b, k1; repeat from * around.

Rnd 3: *P2, p2tog; repeat from * around—24 sts.

Rnd 4: *K1, k1b; repeat from * around.

Rnd 5: *P1, p2tog; repeat from * around—16 sts.

Rnd 6: *K1b, k1; repeat from * around.

Rnd 7: *P2tog; repeat from * around—8 sts.

Finishing

Cut yarn, leaving an 8-in (20.5 cm) tail. Thread yarn needle with end and pick up remaining stitches on knitting needles. Pull tightly to close and secure end. Weave in yarn tails on inside of hat.

Cut twelve 40-in (102 cm) pieces of yarn. Thread 6 pieces through one corner of the hat brim and braid them, held double-stranded. Overhand knot the ends to secure, leaving 2 in (5 cm) of fringe. Repeat on the opposite side.

To make a 2-in (5 cm) pom-pom, hold the three middle fingers of your hand together and wrap working yarn around them until desired thickness. Cut yarn end and cut additional piece of yarn 8 in (20.5 cm) in length. Slide the bundle of yarn off your fingers, tightly pinching the middle of the bundle, wrap the 8-in (20.5 cm) piece of yarn around the middle of the bundle and double knot tightly. Cut through the two end bundles of loops to free the pom-pom pieces. Shape and trim as needed, being careful not to cut the tails of the center knot yarn. Attach pom-pom by threading the long tails through the top of the hat and tying them with a tight knot inside. Trim ends.

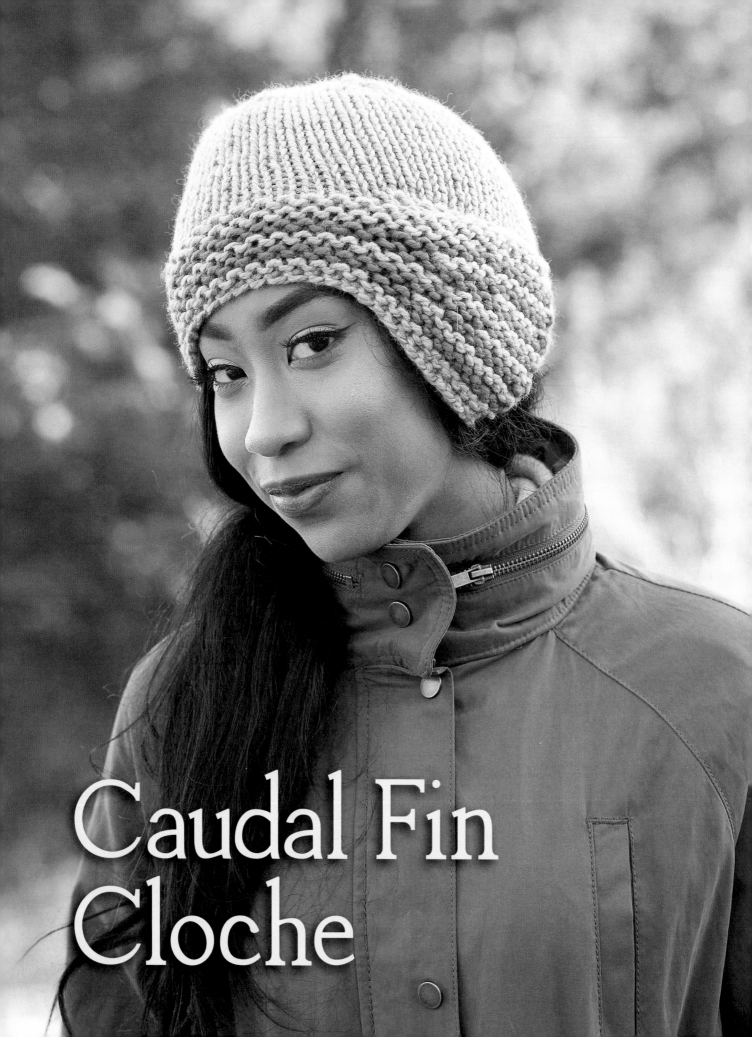

Caudal Fin
Cloche

This nostalgic knit harkens back to 1920s-style cloche hats. An asymmetrical fin detail frames the face in glamorous style. This pattern leaves enough leftover yarn that a second hat could be made in an opposite color motif.

FINISHED MEASUREMENTS

Circumference at brim band, unstretched: 19 in (48 cm); will fit head circumference of 20 to 23 in (50.5 to 58 cm)
- Length from brim edge to crown: 8 in (20 cm)

YARN

MC: 85 yd (78 m) bulky weight #5 yarn; shown knitted in #9452 Summer Sky Heather, Cascade Yarns Cascade 128, 100% Peruvian Highland Wool, 128 yd (117 m) and 3.5 oz (100 g) per skein

CC: 12 yd (11 m) bulky weight #5 yarn; shown knitted in #9553 Ice Blue, Cascade Yarns Cascade 128, 100% Peruvian Highland Wool, 128 yd (117 m) and 3.5 oz (100 g) per skein

NEEDLES AND OTHER MATERIALS

- One 16-in (40.5 cm) circular knitting needle, US 10½ (6.5 mm) or size needed to obtain gauge
- US 10½ (6.5 mm) set of 5 double-pointed needles or size needed to obtain gauge
- Stitch marker
- Scissors
- Yarn needle

GAUGE

12 sts x 18 rows in Stockinette Stitch = 4-in (10 cm) square

NOTES

- Hat brim is worked flat without joining.
- Fin detail is knit in short rows.
- Body of hat and crown shaping is knit in the round. Switch from circular needle to double-pointed needles when necessary during crown shaping.

Brim

Using long-tail method and circular needle, CO
  68 sts in MC. Do not join.
Rows 1 (RS) and 2: With MC, knit.
Rows 3 and 4: With CC, knit 12, turn.
Rows 5 and 6: With MC, knit 10, turn.
Rows 7 and 8: With CC, knit 8, turn.
Rows 9 and 10: With MC, knit 6, turn.
Rows 11 and 12: With CC, knit.
Rows 13 and 14: With MC, knit.
Rows 15 and 16: With CC, knit.
Rows 17 and 18: With MC, knit 6, turn.
Rows 19 and 20: With CC, knit 8, turn.
Rows 21 and 22: With MC, knit 10, turn.
Rows 23 and 24: With CC, knit 12, turn.
Rows 25–28: With MC, knit.
Row 29: Bind off 12 sts. Knit remainder of
  row—56 sts. Join in the round.

Body

Rnds 1–18: Knit.

Crown Shaping

Rnd 1: *K5, k2tog; repeat from * around—48 sts.
Rnd 2: Knit.
Rnd 3: *K4, k2tog; repeat from * around—40 sts.
Rnd 4: Knit.
Rnd 5: *K3, k2tog; repeat from * around—32 sts.
Rnd 6: Knit.
Rnd 7: *K2, k2tog; repeat from * around—24 sts.
Rnd 8: Knit.
Rnd 9: *K1, k2tog; repeat from * around—16 sts.
Rnd 10: Knit.
Rnd 11: *K2tog; repeat from * around—8 sts.

Finishing

Cut yarn, leaving an 8-in (20.5 cm) tail. Thread
  yarn needle with end and pick up remaining
  stitches on knitting needles. Pull tightly to
  close and secure end. Weave in yarn tails on
  inside of hat. Overlap fin detail over brim and
  sew in place.

Wedge Beret

Short rows are nothing to be intimidated by—they are simply rows that are not knit to the end of the needle. This clever knit is constructed sideways on straight needles. Select a yarn with long color repeats to produce this two-tone beret.

FINISHED MEASUREMENTS

Circumference at brim band, unstretched: 18 in (46 cm); will fit head circumference of 20 to 23 in (50.5 to 58 cm)

Length from brim edge to crown: 8¾ in (22 cm)

YARN

90 yd (82 m) bulky weight #5 yarn; shown knitted in #826-209 Charcoal/Aqua, Lion Brand Scarfie, 78% acrylic, 22% wool, 312 yd (285 m) and 5.3 oz (150 g) per skein

NEEDLES AND OTHER MATERIALS

- US 10 (6 mm) set of 2 straight needles or size to obtain gauge
- One US J-10 (6 mm) crochet hook
- Scrap yarn
- Scissors
- Yarn needle

GAUGE

14.5 sts x 18 rows in Stitch Pattern = 4-in (10 cm) square

SPECIAL STITCHES

Knit front and back increase (kfb): Knit into the next stitch, leaving it on the left needle. Bring the tip of the right needle around to the back of the stitch, and knit into the back loop of the same stitch. Slip the stitches off the left needle.

STITCH PATTERN

Short-Row Wedge:

Row 1 (RS): K8, kfb, k20, turn.
Row 2: P22, k8.
Row 3: K8, kfb, k18, turn.
Row 4: P20, k8.
Row 5: K8, kfb, k16, turn.
Row 6: P18, k8.
Row 7: K8, kfb, k14, turn.
Row 8: P16, k8.

Row 9: K8, kfb, k12, turn.
Row 10: P14, k8.
Row 11: K8, kfb, k10, turn.
Row 12: P12, turn.
Row 13: K12, *sl1k, k1, psso, k1; repeat from * to end of row.
Row 14: Sl1p, p23, k8.

NOTES

- Hat is knit flat in short-row wedges, beginning with a provisional cast-on, then seamed with the Kitchener stitch.
- For photo tutorials on the provisional crochet cast-on, knit in front and back increase, and Kitchener stitch, see pages 104, 120, and 126.

Body

Using scrap yarn, the crochet hook, and one of the knitting needles, CO 32 sts using provisional crochet cast-on. Crochet 4 chain sts after cast-on row to easily unravel scrap yarn later. Switch to working yarn, knit first row into live sts on needle.

Rows 1–126: Work entire Short-Row Wedge Pattern 9 times.

Finishing

Cut yarn, leaving 14-in (36 cm) tail. Untie provisional cast-on row scrap yarn and, using free needle, pick up the live stitches from provisional cast-on row. Remove scrap yarn. Be sure both needles are pointing to the right and that the wrong sides of the knitted fabric are facing each other. Thread yarn needle with tail and use the Kitchener stitch to graft stitches together from brim to crown.

Continue until one stitch on each knitting needle remains. Run yarn needle through them both and pick up the top-edge row of stitches at crown. Draw together to close and secure end. Weave in yarn tails on inside of hat.

Sixpence
Cap

Flat cap styles can be traced back to the fourteenth century. They are as fashionable today as they ever were. Innovative construction makes this project easy to adjust.

FINISHED MEASUREMENTS

Small/Medium:

Circumference at brim band, unstretched: 20 in (51 cm); will fit head circumference of 20 to 21 in (50.5 to 53 cm)
Height from bind-off edge to crown: 6 in (15 cm)
Length when laid flat: 10 in (25 cm)
Width when laid flat: 9 in (23 cm)

Large/Extra-Large:

Circumference at brim band, unstretched: 22 in (56 cm); will fit head circumference of 22 to 23 in (56 to 58 cm)
Height from bind-off edge to crown: 6 in (15 cm)
Length when laid flat: 10 in (25 cm)
Width when laid flat: 9 in (23 cm)

YARN

Small/Medium: 70 yd (64 m) super-bulky weight #6 yarn; shown knitted in #640-124 Barley, Lion Brand Wool-Ease Thick & Quick, 80% acrylic, 20% wool, 106 yd (97 m) and 6 oz (170 g) per skein

Large/Extra-Large: 70 yd (64 m) super-bulky weight #6 yarn; shown knitted in #640-123 Oatmeal, Lion Brand Wool-Ease Thick & Quick, 80% acrylic, 20% wool, 106 yd (97 m) and 6 oz (170 g) per skein

NEEDLES AND OTHER MATERIALS
- One 16-in (40.5 cm) circular knitting needle, US 11 (8.0 mm) or size needed to obtain gauge
- Stitch marker
- Scissors
- Yarn needle

GAUGE

9 sts x 20 rows in Garter Stitch = 4-in
(10 cm) square

SPECIAL STITCHES

Make 1 left (M1L) increase: Insert the left needle
from front to back into the horizontal strand
between the stitches on the right and left
needles. Knit the lifted loop through the back.

NOTES

- Hat is knit in three sections: The flat is knit
  without joining, the rise is joined in the round,
  and the brim visor is knit back and forth.
- Pattern is the same for both sizes until round
  10 of the rise.
- For a photo tutorial on the make 1 left
  increase, see page 120.

Flat

Using long-tail method and circular needle,
CO 8 sts. Do not join.
Rows 1–4: Knit.
Row 5: K1, M1L, k6, M1L, k1—10 sts.
Rows 6–8: Knit.
Row 9: K1, M1L, k8, M1L, k1—12 sts.
Rows 10–12: Knit.
Row 13: K1, M1L, k10, M1L, k1—14 sts.
Rows 14–16: Knit.
Row 17: K1, M1L, k12, M1L, k1—16 sts.
Rows 18–32: Knit.
Row 33: K1, k2tog, k10, k2tog, k1—14 sts.
Rows 34–36: Knit.
Row 37: K1, k2tog, k8, k2tog, k1—12 sts.
Rows 38–40: Knit.
Row 41: K1, k2tog, k6, k2tog, k1—10 sts.
Rows 42–44: Knit.
Row 45: K1, k2tog, k4, k2tog, k1—8 sts.
Rows 46–48: Knit.

Rise

Pick up and knit 24 sts along the left edge of
the flat, 8 sts along the back edge, and 24 sts
along the right edge—64 sts. Place marker
and knit in the round.
Rnd 1: Purl.
Rnd 2: Knit.
Rnd 3: Purl.
Rnd 4: Knit.
Rnd 5: Purl.
Rnd 6: *K6, k2tog; repeat from * around—56 sts.
Rnd 7: Purl.
Rnd 8: *K5, k2tog; repeat from * around—48 sts.
Rnd 9: Purl.
Rnd 10 (S/M size only): *K10, k2tog; repeat
from * around—44 sts.
Rnd 10 (L/XL size only): Knit.
Rnd 11: Purl.
Bind off. Cut yarn, leaving a 6-in (15 cm) tail and
draw through last stitch to secure end.

Brim Visor

The short edges of the cap will be the front and
back. Position the cap so the front edge is
farthest from you, and with the inside facing
you, pick up and knit 16 stitches evenly along
the rise edge.
Rows 1–4: Knit.
Row 5: K1, k2tog, k10, k2tog, k1—14 sts.
Row 6: Knit.
Row 7: K1, k2tog, k8, k2tog, k1—12 sts.
Row 8: Knit.
Row 9: K1, k2tog, k6, k2tog, k1—10 sts.
Row 10: Knit.
Bind off. Cut yarn, leaving a 6-in (15 cm) tail and
draw through last stitch to secure end.

Finishing

Fold brim to meet rise and sew flat from
the inside of rise. Weave in yarn tails on
inside of hat.

Olive Branch
Beret

Braided cables twine from a base of neat ribbing to a comfortable gathered crown. The depth and dimension of these thick cable motifs produces a beret with great fullness and loft. Select a plump, solid-colored yarn with good stitch definition.

FINISHED MEASUREMENTS

Circumference at brim band, unstretched: 14 in (36 cm); will fit head circumference of 20 to 23 in (50.5 to 58 cm)

Length from brim edge to crown: 8¾ in (22 cm)

YARN

160 yd (146 m) bulky weight #5 yarn; shown knitted in #671-173 Avocado, Lion Brand Yarn Lion's Pride Woolspun, 80% acrylic, 20% wool, 127 yd (116 m) and 3.5 oz (100 g) per skein

NEEDLES AND OTHER MATERIALS

- One 16-in (40.5 cm) circular knitting needle, US 10½ (6.5 mm)
- One 16-in (40.5 cm) circular knitting needle, US 13 (9.0 mm) or size needed to obtain gauge
- US 13 (9.0 mm) set of 5 double-pointed needles or size needed to obtain gauge
- Stitch marker
- Cable needle
- Scissors
- Yarn needle

GAUGE

14 sts x 16 rows in Cable Stitch Pattern using larger needles (US 13 [9.0 mm] or size needed to obtain gauge) = 4-in (10 cm) square

SPECIAL STITCHES

4/4 right cross (4/4RC): Slip next 4 sts to cable needle, hold cable needle to back of work, knit 4 sts from main needle, knit 4 sts from cable needle.

4/4 left cross (4/4LC): Slip next 4 sts to cable needle, hold cable needle to front of work, knit 4 sts from main needle, knit 4 sts from cable needle.

Knit 1 through the back loop (k1tbl): Holding the working yarn behind the needles, insert the right needle into the back of the first stitch on the left needle from right to left.

Wrap the yarn around the right needle counterclockwise. Pull the yarn through the stitch. Slip the stitch off the left needle.

Make 1 left (M1L) increase: Insert the left needle from front to back into the horizontal strand between the stitches on the right and left needles. Knit the lifted loop through the back.

STITCH PATTERN

Cable Stitch Pattern:

Rnd 1: *K12, p2; repeat from * around.
Rnd 2: *K12, p2; repeat from * around.
Rnd 3: *4/4LC, k4, p2; repeat from * around.
Rnd 4: *K12, p2; repeat from * around.
Rnd 5: *K12, p2; repeat from * around.
Rnd 6: *K12, p2; repeat from * around.
Rnd 7: *K4, 4/4RC, p2; repeat from * around.
Rnd 8: *K12, p2; repeat from * around.

NOTES

- Hat is worked in rounds from bottom edge to crown. Switch from circular needles to double-pointed needles when necessary during crown shaping.
- For photo tutorials on working knit 1 through the back loop, 4/4 left cross, 4/4 right cross, and make 1 left increase, see pages 109, 114, 115, and 120.

Brim

Using long-tail method and US 10½ (6.5 mm) circular needle, CO 56 sts. Place a stitch marker between first and last sts and join in the round, being careful not to twist the cast-on row.

Rnds 1–8: *K1tbl, p1; repeat from * around.
Rnd 9: Using US 13 (9.0 mm) circular needle, *k1, M1L; repeat from *around—112 sts.

Body

Rnds 1–24: Work entire Cable Stitch Pattern 3 times.

Crown Shaping

Rnd 1: *Ssk twice, k2tog four times, p2; repeat from * around—64 sts.
Rnd 2: *K6, p2; repeat from * around.
Rnd 3: *Ssk, k2tog twice, p2; repeat from * around—40 sts.
Rnd 4: *K3, p2; repeat from * around.
Rnd 5: *K3tog, p2tog; repeat from * around—16 sts.
Rnd 6: *K2tog; repeat from * around—8 sts.

Finishing

Cut yarn, leaving an 8-in (20.5 cm) tail. Thread yarn needle with end and pick up remaining stitches on knitting needles. Pull tightly to close and secure end. Weave in yarn tails on inside of hat.

Café au Lait
Beaded Beanie

Coffee bean–shaped beads nest in a foamy froth of smocked stitches. This distinctive look is an excellent introduction into the art of beaded knitting. Each bead is strung individually with the aid of a thin crochet hook.

FINISHED MEASUREMENTS

Circumference at brim band, unstretched: 17 in (43 cm); will fit head circumference of 20 to 23 in (50.5 to 58 cm)
Length from brim edge to crown: 8 in (20 cm)

YARN

100 yd (91 m) bulky weight #5 yarn; shown knitted in #671-099 Linen, Lion Brand Yarn Lion's Pride Woolspun, 80% acrylic, 20% wool, 127 yd (116 m) and 3.5 oz (100 g) per skein

NEEDLES AND OTHER MATERIALS

- One 16-in (40.5 cm) circular knitting needle, US 10½ (6.5 mm) or size needed to obtain gauge
- US 10½ (6.5 mm) set of 5 double-pointed needles or size needed to obtain gauge
- 64 12 mm long x 8 mm wide wooden beads with 3 mm bead holes
- Stitch marker
- 2.0 mm crochet hook
- Scissors
- Yarn needle

GAUGE

14 sts x 20 rows in Stitch Pattern = 4-in (10 cm) square

SPECIAL STITCHES

Smocking stitch (Smk): Insert right needle between second and third stitch, draw up a loop of working yarn on the right needle.
Smocking stitch with bead (Smkb): Insert right needle between second and third stitch, draw up a loop of working yarn, hold loop with crochet hook, and string bead over hook and onto loop, place loop onto right needle.

STITCH PATTERN

Rnd 1: *Smk, k4, Smkb, k4; repeat from * around—80 sts.
Rnd 2: *K2tog, k3; repeat from * around—64 sts.

Rnd 3: K2, *Smk, k4; repeat from * until last 2 sts, Smk, k2—80 sts.

Rnd 4: K2, *k2tog, k3; repeat from * until last 3 sts, k2tog, k1—64 sts.

Rnd 5: *Smkb, k4, Smk, k4; repeat from * around—80 sts.

Rnd 6: *K2tog, k3; repeat from * around—64 sts.

Rnd 7: K2, *Smk, k4; repeat from * until last 2 sts, Smk, k2—80 sts.

Rnd 8: K2, *k2tog, k3; repeat from * until last 3 sts, k2tog, k2—64 sts.

NOTES

- Hat is worked in rounds from bottom edge to crown. Switch from circular needles to double-pointed needles when necessary during crown shaping.
- Be certain to choose a crochet hook with a slender shaft that allows the bead to slip all the way over it.
- For a photo tutorial on the smocking stitch and smocking stitch with bead, see page 117.

Brim

Using long-tail method and US 10½ (6.5 mm) circular needle, CO 64 sts. Place a stitch marker between first and last sts and join in the round, being careful not to twist the cast-on row.

Rnds 1–8: *K2, p2; repeat from * around.

Body

Rnds 1–16: Work entire Stitch Pattern 2 times.

Rnds 17–20: Work rnds 1–4 of Stitch Pattern.

Crown Shaping

Rnd 1: *Smkb, k4, Smk, k2, k2tog; repeat from * around—72 sts.

Rnd 2: *K2tog, k3, k2tog, k2; repeat from * around—56 sts.

Rnd 3: K2tog, *Smk, k5, k2tog; repeat from * until last 5 sts, Smk, k5.

Rnd 4: K1, *k2tog, k5; repeat from * until last 6 sts, k2tog, k4—48 sts.

Rnd 5: *K2tog, k2, Smkb, k2; repeat from * around.

Rnd 6: K3, *k2tog, k4; repeat from * until last 3 sts, k2tog, k1—40 sts.

Rnd 7: *K3, k2tog; repeat from * around—32 sts.

Rnd 8: *K2, k2tog; repeat from * around—24 sts.

Rnd 9: *Smkb, k3; repeat from * around—32 sts.

Rnd 10: *K2tog; repeat from * around—16 sts.

Rnd 11: *K2tog; repeat from * around—8 sts.

Finishing

Cut yarn, leaving an 8-in (20.5 cm) tail. Thread yarn needle with end and pick up remaining stitches on knitting needles. Pull tightly to close and secure end. Weave in yarn tails on inside of hat.

Moorland Heather Beanie

The rise and fall of windswept highlands is mimicked in the peak-and-valley ribbing of this snug beanie. Fields of reverse stockinette reflect foggy purple flowers among the grass and bracken. Quartered decreases create an architectural crown with subtle details.

FINISHED MEASUREMENTS
Circumference at brim band, unstretched: 16 in (41 cm); will fit head circumference of 20 to 23 in (50.5 to 58 cm)
Length from brim edge to crown: 8½ in (22 cm)

YARN
95 yd (87 m) bulky weight #5 yarn; shown knitted in #26388 Seraphim, Knit Picks Brava Bulky, 100% premium acrylic, 136 yd (124 m) and 3.5 oz (100 g) per skein

NEEDLES AND OTHER MATERIALS
- One 16-in (40.5 cm) circular knitting needle, US 10½ (6.5 mm) or size needed to obtain gauge
- US 10½ (6.5 mm) set of 5 double-pointed needles or size needed to obtain gauge
- Stitch marker
- Scissors
- Yarn needle
- Three ½ in (1.25 cm) buttons

GAUGE
14 sts x 20 rows in Reverse Stockinette Stitch = 4-in (10 cm) square

NOTES
- Hat is worked in rounds from bottom edge to crown. Switch from circular needles to double-pointed needles when necessary during crown shaping.

Brim

Using long-tail method and circular needles, CO 72 sts. Place a stitch marker between first and last sts and join in the round, being careful not to twist the cast-on row.

Rnds 1–18: Work entire chart for 18 rounds, or, if you prefer written instructions, follow the instructions below.

Rnds 1 and 2: *K1, p1; repeat from * around.

Rnds 3 and 4: *(K1, p1) 7 times, k1, p5, (k1, p1) 8 times; repeat from *.

Rnds 5 and 6: *(K1, p1) 6 times, k1, p9, (k1, p1) 7 times; repeat from *.

Rnds 7 and 8: *(K1, p1) 5 times, k1, p13, (k1, p1) 6 times; repeat from *.

Rnds 9 and 10: *(K1, p1) 4 times, k1, p17, (k1, p1) 5 times; repeat from *.

Rnds 11 and 12: *(K1, p1) 3 times, k1, p21, (k1, p1) 4 times; repeat from *.

Rnds 13 and 14: *(K1, p1) 2 times, k1, p25, (k1, p1) 3 times; repeat from *.

Rnds 15 and 16: *K1, p1, k1, p29, (k1, p1) twice; repeat from *.

Rnds 17 and 18: *K1, p33, k1, p1; repeat from *.

Body

Rnds 1–8: Purl.

Rnd 9: Purl until last 3 sts, sl3p, remove stitch marker, move 3 slipped stitches back to left needle, place marker.

Crown Shaping

Rnd 1: *Ssk, p1, k2tog, p13; rep from * around—64 sts.

Rnd 2: *K1, p1, k1, p13; rep from * around until the last 16 sts, k1, p1, k1, p12, sl1p, remove stitch marker, move slipped stitch back to left needle, place marker.

Rnd 3: *Ssk, p1, k2tog, p11; rep from * around—56 sts.

Rnd 4: *K1, p1, k1, p11; rep from * around until the last 14 sts, k1, p1, k1, p10, sl1p, remove stitch marker, move slipped stitch back to left needle, place marker.

Rnd 5: *Ssk, p1, k2tog, p9; rep from * around—48 sts.

Rnd 6: *K1, p1, k1, p9; rep from * around until the last 12 sts, k1, p1, k1, p8, sl1p, remove

Chart 1

	Knit
●	Purl

stitch marker, move slipped stitch back to left needle, place marker.

Rnd 7: *Ssk, p1, k2tog, p7; rep from * around—40 sts.

Rnd 8: *K1, p1, k1, p7; rep from * around until the last 10 sts, k1, p1, k1, p6, sl1p, remove stitch marker, move slipped stitch back to left needle, place marker.

Rnd 9: *Ssk, p1, k2tog, p5; rep from * around—32 sts.

Rnd 10: *K1, p1, k1, p5; rep from * around until the last 8 sts, k1, p1, k1, p4, sl1p, remove stitch marker, move slipped stitch back to left needle, place marker.

Rnd 11: *Ssk, p1, k2tog, p3; rep from * around—24 sts.

Rnd 12: *K1, p1, k1, p3; rep from * around until the last 6 sts, k1, p1, k1, p2, sl1p, remove stitch marker, move slipped stitch back to left needle, place marker.

Rnd 13: *Ssk, p1, k2tog, p1; rep from * around—16 sts.

Rnd 14: *Ssk, k2tog; rep from * around—8 sts.

Finishing

Cut yarn, leaving an 8-in (20.5 cm) tail. Thread yarn needle with end and pick up remaining stitches on knitting needles. Pull tightly to close and secure end. Weave in yarn tails on inside of hat. Sew buttons securely in place.

Rusty Rooster
Lace Beanie

This cap is proof-positive that lace knitting is as glorious in bulky yarns as it is in thin, gauzy yarns. The eyelet panels, resembling rooster combs, elegantly decrease toward the crown. A slight haze cast by the alpaca-blend yarn embodies the rustic spirit of this jaunty beanie.

FINISHED MEASUREMENTS
Circumference at brim band, unstretched: 16 in (41 cm); will fit head circumference of 20 to 23 in (50.5 to 58 cm)
Length from brim edge to crown: 8 in (20 cm)

YARN
90 yd (82 m) bulky weight #5 yarn; shown knitted in #18 Copper, Valley Yarns Berkshire Bulky, 85% wool, 15% alpaca, 108 yd (99 m) and 3.5 oz (100 g) per skein

NEEDLES AND OTHER MATERIALS
- One 16-in (40.5 cm) circular knitting needle, US 10½ (6.5 mm) or size needed to obtain gauge
- US 10½ (6.5 mm) set of 5 double-pointed needles or size needed to obtain gauge
- Stitch marker
- Scissors
- Yarn needle

GAUGE
15 sts x 18 rows in Stitch Pattern = 4-in (10 cm) square

SPECIAL STITCHES
Knit 4 together decrease (k4tog): Insert the right needle into the first four stitches on the left needle. Knit these stitches together as though they are one stitch.
Make 1 left (M1L) increase: Insert the left needle from front to back into the horizontal strand between the stitches on the right and left needles. Knit the lifted loop through the back.

STITCH PATTERN
Rnds 1 and 2: *K13, p1; rep from * around.
Rnd 3: *K4tog, (yo, k1) 5 times, yo, k4tog, p1; rep from * around.
Rnd 4: Repeat rnd 1.

Brim

Using long-tail method and circular needles, CO 60 sts. Place a stitch marker between first and last sts and join in the round, being careful not to twist the cast-on row.

Rnds 1–10: *K1, p1; rep from * around.
Rnd 11: *K2, M1L, k3, M1L; rep from * around—84 sts.

Body

Rnds 1–16: Work entire Stitch Pattern 4 times.

Crown Shaping

Rnds 1 and 2: *K13, p1; rep from * around.
Rnd 3: *K4tog, k1, (yo, k1) 4 times, k4tog, p1; rep from * around—72 sts.
Rnd 4: *K11, p1; rep from * around.
Rnd 5: *K1, k2tog, k5, k2tog, k1, p1; rep from * around—60 sts.
Rnd 6: *K9, p1; rep from * around.
Rnd 7: *K4tog, yo, k1, yo, k4tog, p1; rep from * around—36 sts.
Rnd 8: *K5, p1; rep from * around.
Rnd 9: *K2tog, k1, k2tog, p1; rep from * around—24 sts.
Rnd 10: *K3, p1; rep from * around.
Rnd 11: *K4tog; rep from * around—6 sts.

Finishing

Cut yarn, leaving an 8-in (20.5 cm) tail. Thread yarn needle with end and pick up remaining stitches on knitting needles. Pull tightly to close and secure end. Weave in yarn tails on inside of hat.

NOTES

- Hat is worked in rounds from bottom edge to crown. Switch from circular needles to double-pointed needles when necessary during crown shaping.
- For photo tutorials on the make 1 left increase and knit 4 together decrease, see pages 120 and 121.

Stitches and Techniques

The purpose of this section is to provide written and visual instructions for the knitting techniques covered in this book. From casting on to binding off, following these simple step-by-step instructions should make even the most intimidating of patterns a piece of cake.

Casting On

To begin a project, you must cast the yarn onto knitting needles, creating a base row of stitches on which to build. There are dozens of different ways of casting on, but I will focus on three used in this book: the long-tail cast-on, two-color cast-on, and the provisional crochet cast-on.

LONG-TAIL CAST-ON

My go-to cast-on is the long-tail cast-on. I think it is the easiest to learn and creates a nice stable medium-stretch row that is easy to knit into. Begin by estimating how much yarn is needed for the long tail. It should include roughly 1 inch of yarn per cast-on stitch, plus 6 to 8 inches for weaving in when the garment is finished.

1. Position your hand as though it is holding an invisible slingshot. Drape the yarn over your hand with the long tail end over the thumb and the working yarn over the index finger. Gather these two strands in your palm with your other three fingers. Do not hold this yarn too tightly; as you build the row, these strands will need to flow with an even tension.

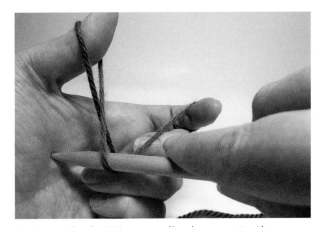

2. Press the knitting needle down onto the length of yarn that is between the thumb and index finger to form a V.

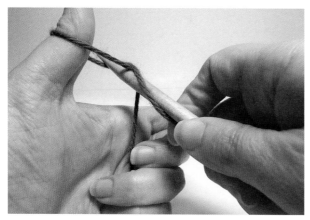

3. Bring the needle up into the loop that has been formed around the thumb.

4. Turn your wrist so that your thumb is now pointing at you, and use the needle to scoop up the length of yarn that is strung between the index finger and palm.

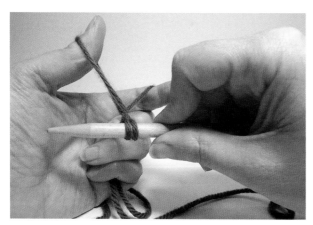

5. Tilt the needle back down into the loop around the thumb.

6. Let go of the yarn around the thumb and pull down on the tail end to snug the loop to the needle. Avoid tightening the stitch too much. Following these steps the first time will result in two stitches on the needle.

7. Repeat steps 3–6 for each additional stitch.

TWO-COLOR CAST-ON

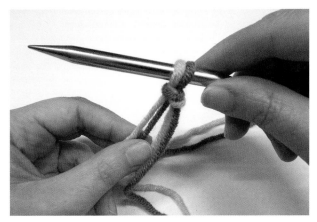

1. With one strand of each color, form a slipknot and place it on the knitting needle. This loop is temporary and will be removed. Do not count this loop as a stitch.

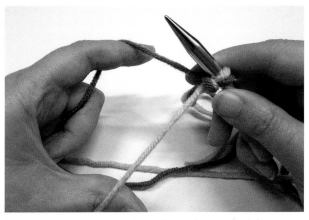

2. Position your hand as though it is holding an invisible slingshot. Drape the yarn over your hand with the main color over the thumb and the contrasting color over the index finger. Gather these two strands in your palm with your other three fingers. Do not hold this yarn too tightly; as you build the row, these strands will need to flow with an even tension.

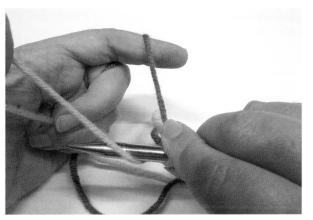

3. Press the knitting needle down onto the length of yarn that is between the thumb and index finger to form a V.

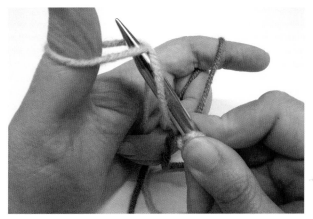

4. Bring the needle up into the loop that has been formed around the thumb.

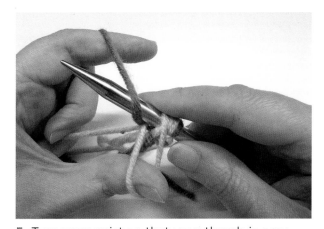

5. Turn your wrist so that your thumb is now pointing at you and use the needle to scoop up the length of yarn that is strung between the index finger and palm.

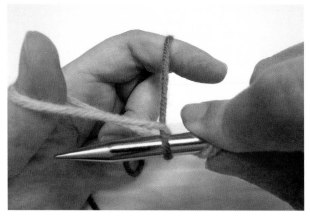

6. Tilt the needle back down into the loop around the thumb.

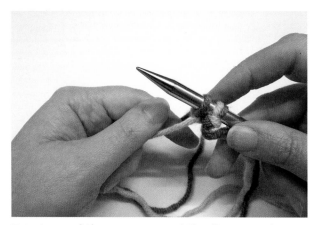

7. Let go of the yarn around the finger and thumb and pull down on the tail ends to snug the loop to the needle. Avoid tightening the stitch too much.

8. Repeat these steps for each additional stitch.

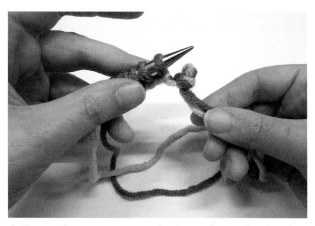

9. Drop the temporary slip knot from the back end of the needle.

PROVISIONAL CROCHET CAST-ON

A provisional crochet cast-on is worked over a scrap piece of yarn that will later be removed to expose live stitches. These live stitches can then be worked from seamlessly. This is helpful when a project requires that a beginning edge and finished edge should be invisibly seamed together.

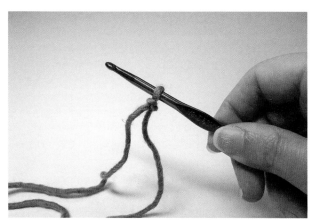

1. Create a slipknot with the scrap yarn and place it on the crochet hook.

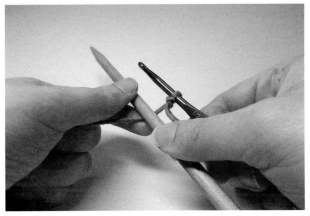

2. Hold the knitting needle in your left hand and the crochet hook in your right hand, with the working end of the scrap yarn behind the needle.

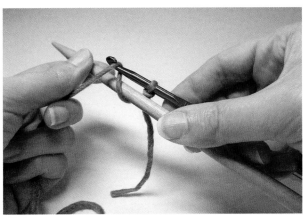

3. Hook the scrap yarn with your crochet hook, covering the knitting needle.

4. Draw the yarn through the loop on the hook, encasing the knitting needle in a loop of yarn.

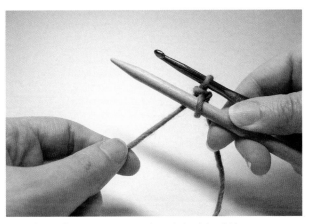

5. Bring the scrap yarn back behind the knitting needle.

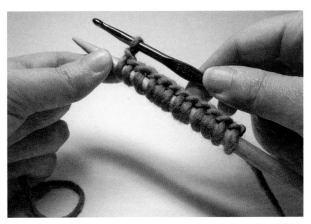

6. Repeat these steps for each additional stitch.

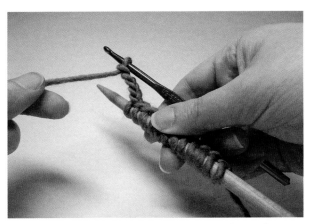

7. Crochet chain four additional stitches after the cast-on row so you can readily identify which end to unravel later.

8. Cut tail and secure the loose end.

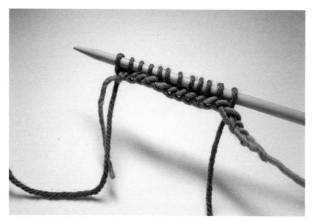

9. Switch to the working yarn and knit across the crochet stitches. Continue the project as written.

10. To remove the provisional cast-on, begin by untying the knot in the scrap yarn at the end with the four additional crochet stitches.

11. Unravel the extra stitches.

12. Unravel the first stitch, exposing the live stitch.

13. Insert a knitting needle into the live stitch, where the scrap yarn was.

14. Continue down the row, exposing each live stitch and inserting the needle into it until the row is completely on the needle and free of the scrap yarn.

Basic Stitches

Knitted fabric is made up of interlocking building blocks that create length, width, and texture. Patterns will call for different configurations of these blocks to create the finished piece. Learning the basics is essential, as well as a few variations on these techniques.

KNIT (K)

1. Holding the working yarn behind the needles, insert the right needle into the front of the first stitch on the left needle from left to right.

2. Wrap the yarn around the right needle counterclockwise.

3. Pull the yarn through the stitch.

4. Slip the stitch off the left needle onto the right needle.

PURL (P)

1. Holding the working yarn in front of your needles, insert the right needle into the front of the first stitch on the left needle from right to left.

2. Wrap the yarn around the right needle counterclockwise.

3. Pull the yarn through the stitch.

4. Slip the stitch off the left needle.

YARN OVER (YO)

1. Wrap the yarn around the right needle counterclockwise. Continue to knit as normal.

SLIP 1 KNITWISE (SL1K)

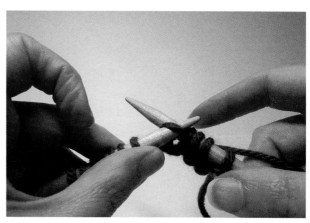

1. Insert the right needle into the first stitch on the left needle as if to knit.

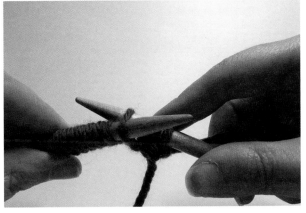

KNIT 1 THROUGH THE BACK LOOP (K1TBL)

2. Slide the stitch off the left needle onto the right needle.

1. Holding the working yarn behind the needles, insert the right needle into the back of the first stitch on the left needle from right to left.

SLIP 1 PURLWISE (SL1P)

1. Insert the right needle into the first stitch on the left needle as if to purl.

2. Wrap the yarn around the right needle counterclockwise.

2. Slide the stitch off the left needle onto the right needle.

3. Pull the yarn through the stitch.

4. Slip the stitch off the left needle.

KNIT 1 BELOW (K1B)

1. Holding the working yarn behind the needles, insert the right needle into the front of the first stitch directly below the next stitch on the left needle.

2. Wrap the yarn around the right needle counterclockwise.

3. Pull the yarn though the stitch.

4. Slip the stitch off the left needle.

KNIT 2 BELOW (K2B)

1. Holding the working yarn behind the needles, insert the right needle into the front of the first stitch two rows below the next stitch on the left needle.

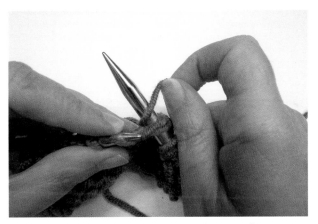

2. Wrap the yarn around the right needle counterclockwise.

3. Pull the yarn though the stitch.

4. Slip the stitch off the left needle.

Cables and Texture Stitches

Put simply, knitted cables are achieved by knitting stitches out of order, crossing layers of knitted fabric over one another. Textures are accomplished by manipulating basic stitches, sometimes in a slightly unusual way. Both techniques can turn a very basic project into something extraordinary.

RIGHT TWIST (RT)

1. Insert the right needle into second stitch on the left needle knitwise.

2. Wrap the working yarn around the right needle counterclockwise.

3. Pull the working yarn through the stitch, leaving the stitch on the needle.

4. Insert the right needle into the first stitch on the left needle knitwise.

5. Wrap the working yarn around the right needle counterclockwise.

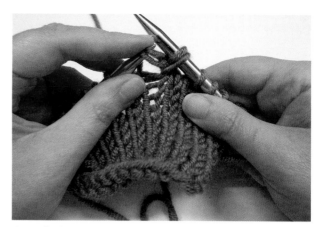

6. Pull the working yarn through the stitch, sliding both stitches off the left needle.

2/2 RIGHT CROSS (2/2 RC)

1. Slip next 2 stitches to a cable needle.

2. Hold the cable needle to the back of the work.

3. Knit 2 stitches from the main needle.

4. Knit 2 stitches from the cable needle.

5. Completed 2/2 Right Cross.

3/3 RIGHT CROSS (3/3 RC)

1. Slip next 3 stitches to a cable needle.

2. Hold the cable needle to the back of the work.

3. Knit 3 stitches from the main needle.

4. Knit 3 stitches from the cable needle.

2. Hold the cable needle to the front of the work.

5. Completed 3/3 Right Cross.

3. Knit 4 stitches from the main needle.

4/4 LEFT CROSS (4/4 LC)

1. Slip next 4 stitches to a cable needle.

4. Knit 4 stitches from the cable needle.

5. Completed 4/4 Left Cross.

4/4 RIGHT CROSS (4/4 RC)

1. Slip next 4 stitches to a cable needle.

2. Hold the cable needle to the back of the work.

3. Knit 4 stitches from the main needle.

4. Knit 4 stitches from the cable needle.

5. Completed 4/4 Right Cross.

I-CORD

1. Using long-tail method and 2 double-pointed needles, cast on 4 stitches.

2. Knit across.

3. Slide the work to the right end of the double-pointed needle. Do not turn the work.

4. With the working yarn coming around the back from the left-most stitch, knit into the right-most stitch and continue knitting the row.

5. Repeat steps 3 and 4 until desired length.

SMOCKING STITCH (SMK)

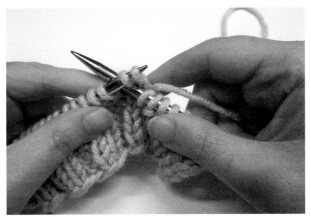

1. Insert right needle between second and third stitch on left needle.

2. Wrap the right needle with the working yarn counterclockwise.

3. Pull a loop of working yarn through and leave it on the right needle.

SMOCKING STITCH WITH BEAD (SMKB)

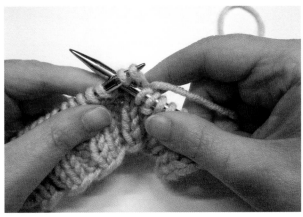

1. Insert right needle between second and third stitch on left needle.

2. Wrap the right needle with the working yarn counterclockwise.

3. Pull a loop of working yarn through.

4. Hold loop with crochet hook.

5. String bead over hook and onto loop.

6. Place loop on the right needle.

ELONGATED LOOP LEFT (ELL)

1. Insert right needle into center of second knit stitch of previous 3 knit rib four rows below.

2. Wrap the right needle with the working yarn counterclockwise.

3. Pull up a loop of working yarn onto the right needle.

ELONGATED LOOP RIGHT (ELR)

1. Insert right needle into center of second knit stitch of next 3 knit rib four rows below.

2. Wrap the right needle with the working yarn counterclockwise.

3. Pull up a loop of working yarn onto the right needle.

POPCORN STITCH (PCS)

1. Holding the working yarn behind the needles, knit into the next stitch, leaving it on the left needle.

2. Holding the working yarn in front of your needles, purl into the same stitch, leaving it on the left needle.

3. Holding the working yarn behind the needles, knit into the same stitch, leaving it on the left needle.

4. Holding the working yarn in front of your needles, purl into the same stitch, slip the stitch off the left needle.

Shaping: Increases and Decreases

Increasing and decreasing the number of stitches in a row will allow you to alter the shape of knitting. Typically, in this book, I will use increases to add more volume to a hat and decreases to slope a crown.

MAKE 1 LEFT INCREASE (M1L)

This make 1 increase creates a smooth new left-leaning knit stitch between two other stitches. This is an easy general increase that adds width without leaving a large hole or loop.

1. Insert the left needle from front to back into the horizontal strand between the stitches on the right and left needles.

2. Knit the lifted loop through the back. Knit as usual.

KNIT FRONT AND BACK INCREASE (KFB)

This increase will leave you with a decorative bar at the base of the second stitch.

1. Knit into the next stitch, leaving it on the left needle.

2. Bring the tip of the right needle around to the back of the stitch and knit into the back loop of the same stitch.

3. Slip the stitches off the left needle.

KNIT 2 TOGETHER DECREASE (K2TOG)

This is probably the most commonly used decrease. It creates a decrease that slants to the right.

1. Insert the right needle into the first two stitches on the left needle as if to knit.

2. Knit these stitches together as though they are one stitch.

KNIT 4 TOGETHER DECREASE (K4TOG)

1. Insert the right needle into the first four stitches on the left needle as if to purl.

2. Knit these stitches together as though they are one stitch.

PURL 2 TOGETHER DECREASE (P2TOG)

1. Insert the right needle into the first two stitches on the left needle as if to purl.

2. Purl these stitches together as though they are one stitch.

PURL 3 TOGETHER DECREASE (P3TOG)

1. Insert the right needle into the first three stitches on the left needle as if to purl.

2. Purl these stitches together as though they are one stitch.

SLIP, SLIP, KNIT DECREASE (SSK)

This decrease slants to the left.

1. Use the tip of your right needle to slip the first stitch off the left needle knitwise.

2. Use the tip of your right needle to slip the second stitch off the left needle knitwise.

3. Insert the left needle into these two stitches on the right needle.

4. Knit these stitches together as though they are one stitch.

SLIP 1 KNITWISE, KNIT 1, PASS SLIPPED STITCH OVER DECREASE (SL1K, K1, PSSO)

1. Use the tip of your right needle to slip the first stitch off the left needle knitwise.

2. Knit the next stitch.

3. Pass the slipped stitch on the right needle over the knitted stitch and off the needle.

SLIP 1 KNITWISE, KNIT 2, PASS SLIPPED STITCH OVER DECREASE (SL1K, K2, PSSO)

1. Use the tip of your right needle to slip the first stitch off the left needle knitwise.

2. Knit the next two stitches.

3. Pass the slipped stitch on the right needle over the two knitted stitches and off the needle.

SLIP 2 *TOGETHER* KNITWISE, KNIT 1, PASS SLIPPED STITCHES OVER DECREASE (S2KP2)

1. Use the tip of your right needle to slip the first two stitches together off the left needle knitwise.

2. Knit the next stitch.

3. Pass the slipped stitches on the right needle over the knitted stitch and off the needle.

Finishing

Securing your new project from unraveling is of utmost importance. First, you must get it off the needles. Binding off your knitting is a process of ending each column of stitches and providing a finished edge or gather. This section will also cover how to join two live rows for a nearly invisible seam.

CINCHING UP A HAT

This is truly the easiest technique possible for securing the crown of a hat.

1. Cut the yarn, leaving an 8-in (20.5 cm) tail.

2. Thread a yarn needle with the end and pick up the remaining stitches on the knitting needle(s).

3. Pull tightly to close and secure the end.

4. Weave in the yarn tail on the inside of the hat.

BINDING OFF (BO)

When simply instructed to bind off, this is the method to use.

1. Knit 2 stitches.

2. Insert the tip of the left needle into the far right stitch on the right needle.

3. Lift the stitch up and over the left stitch on the right needle and off the needle.

4. Knit the next stitch on the left needle.

5. Repeat steps 2–4 until all stitches are bound. Cut the yarn leaving an 8 in (20.5 cm) tail and secure it through the remaining loop on the right needle.

THE KITCHENER STITCH

The Kitchener stitch is a way of grafting two live rows of knitting together from the outside of the work to form an almost invisible seam.

1. First you will need to do an anchor row. Hold your needles parallel, pointing toward the right. Cut your working yarn, leaving a tail one and a half times the length of the seam. Thread a yarn needle and insert it into the first stitch of the front needle as if to purl and draw the yarn through, leaving the stitch on the knitting needle.

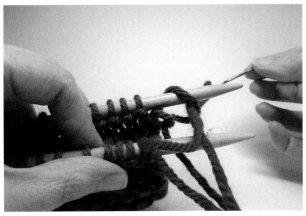

2. Now insert the yarn needle into the first stitch on the back knitting needle as if to knit; draw the yarn through, leaving the stitch on the knitting needle.

5. Insert the yarn needle into the first stitch of the back knitting needle as if to purl and draw the yarn through. Slip this stitch off the knitting needle.

3. Now we will begin the process of grafting. Insert the yarn needle into the first stitch of the front knitting needle as if to knit and draw the yarn through. Slip this stitch off the knitting needle.

6. Insert the yarn needle into the second stitch of the back knitting needle as if to knit and draw the yarn through. Leave this stitch on the knitting needle.

4. Insert the yarn needle into the second stitch of the front knitting needle as if to purl and draw the yarn through. Leave this stitch on the knitting needle.

7. Repeat steps 3–6 to continue grafting the live stitches together, occasionally tugging your tail yarn to tighten.

Embellishments

Embellishments can add a great deal of character and personality to a piece. Pom-poms and tassels serve a double purpose, in that they can also add weight to hold down otherwise floppy strips of knitted fabric. They're also an ideal way of using up the leftover bits of yarn from your project.

POM-POMS

1. To make a 2-in (5 cm) pom-pom, hold the three middle fingers of your hand together and wrap yarn around them until the desired thickness.

2. Cut the yarn end and cut another piece of yarn about 8 in (20.5 cm) in length.

3. Slide the bundle of yarn off your fingers, tightly pinching the middle of the bundle. Wrap the 8-in (20.5 cm) piece of yarn around the middle of the bundle three times and double knot tightly.

4. Cut through the two end bundles of loops to free the pom-pom pieces.

5. Shape and trim as needed, being careful not to cut the tails of the center knot yarn. Attach the pom-pom by tying its long tails into the knitting. Trim ends.

TASSELS

1. To make a 6-in (15 cm) tassel, cut a 6-in (15 cm) long piece of cardboard.

2. Cut two pieces of yarn 13 in (33 cm) each and set aside.

3. Wrap the working yarn around the cardboard 30 or more times, depending on how thick you would like the tassel to be, and cut the end of yarn on the same side where the wrapping began.

4. Slide one of the 13-in (33 cm) pieces of yarn under the opposite end and double-knot tightly.

5. Slide scissors between the cardboard and the yarn at the opposite end and cut the yarn to free the tassel.

6. Hold the tassel firmly and wrap the second 13-in (33 cm) piece of yarn around the bundle twice about 1 in (2.5 cm) from the top knot and double-knot tightly.

When attaching to the project, feed the top knot tails through the tip of the hat and secure, then use the yarn needle to feed those ends down through the tassel. Trim ends as needed.

Abbreviations

2/2 RC	two over two right cross		**P2tog**	purl two stitches together
3/3 RC	three over three right cross		**P3tog**	purl three stitches together
4/4 LC	four over four left cross		**PSSO**	pass slipped stitch over
4/4 RC	four over four right cross		**Rep**	repeat
BO	bind off		**Rnd(s)**	round(s)
CC	contrasting color		**RS**	right side of knitted fabric
CO	cast on		**RT**	right twist
Dpn(s)	double-pointed needle(s)		**S2kp2**	slip two stitches together, knit 1 stitch, pass two slipped stitches over the knit stitch
Drop 1	drop next stitch from left needle			
K	knit		**Sl**	slip
K1b	knit one stitch below		**Sl1k**	slip one stitch as if to knit
K1tlb	knit one stitch through the back loop		**Sl1p**	slip one stitch as if to purl
			Smk	smocking stitch
K2tog	knit two stitches together		**Smkb**	smocking stitch with a bead
K4tog	knit four stitches together		**Ssk**	slip slip knit decrease
Kfb	knit into front and back of the stitch to increase		**St(s)**	stitch(es)
			WS	wrong side of knitted fabric
MC	main color		**Yd**	yard(s)
M1L	left-leaning make one increase		**YO**	yarn over
P	purl			

Yarn Sources

BERROCO
berroco.com

BROWN SHEEP COMPANY
brownsheep.com

CASCADE YARNS
cascadeyarns.com

KNIT PICKS
knitpicks.com

LION BRAND
lionbrand.com

LOOPS & THREADS
michaels.com

MADELINETOSH
madelinetosh.com

MALABRIGO
malabrigoyarn.com

PATONS
yarnspirations.com

VALLEY YARN
valleyyarn.com

WILLOW YARNS
willowyarns.com

Stitch and Technique Index

Visual Index

Beanstalks Slouchy Hat

4

Iron Lion Cloche

7

Twisting Streams Beret

11

Dewdrops Beanie

14

Wildflower Fields Beanie

17

Red Vine Cable Beanie

20

Wood Nymph Hat

23

Lake Bonnet

27

Marigold Slouchy Hat

30

Mama Bear Hooded Cowl
33

Baby Bear Hooded Cowl
36

Conch Beret
39

Hyacinth Bow Beret
42

Nubbins Slouchy Hat
45

Pine Hill Drive Beret
48

Ombre Marled Pixie Hood
52

Kilderkin Beanie
55

Driftwood Wrap Hood
58

Latvian Lampreys Hat
61

Parquet Slouchy Beanie
65

Braided Cable Hood
68

Bougainvillea Beret
72

Honeycomb Split Brim Beanie
75

Caudal Fin Cloche
78

Wedge Beret
81

Sixpence Cap
84

Olive Branch Beret
88

Café au Lait Beaded Beanie
91

Moorland Heather Beanie
94

Rusty Rooster Lace Beanie
98